GRETEL EHRLICH

THE FUTURE OF ICE

Gretel Ehrlich is the author of *This Cold Heaven* and *The Solace of Open Spaces*, among other works of nonfiction, fiction, and poetry. She divides her time between California and Wyoming.

# THE FUTURE OF ICE

# THE FUTURE OF ICE

*A Journey into Cold*

GRETEL EHRLICH

*Vintage Books*
*A Division of Random House, Inc.*
*New York*

FIRST VINTAGE BOOKS EDITION, NOVEMBER 2005

Grateful acknowledgment is made to Copper Canyon Press for permission to reprint
an excerpt from "At Whole-World-In-View Hut," by Muso Soseki, translated by
W. S. Merwin from *East Window: The Asian Translations*. Copyright © 1998 by

Port Townsend, WA 98368-0271.

The Library of Congress has cataloged the Pantheon edition as follows:
Ehrlich, Gretel.
The future of ice : a journey into cold / Gretel Ehrlich.
p. cm.
1. Ehrlich, Gretel—Travel—Cold regions.  2. Cold regions—Description and travel.
3. Cold—Psychological aspects.  4. Weather—Psychological aspects.  I. Title.
G465.E46 2004    818'.5403—dc22    2004044666

Vintage ISBN-10: 1-4000-3435-3
Vintage ISBN-13: 978-1-4000-3435-2

Author photograph © Rita Donham
Book design by M. Kristen Bearse

www.vintagebooks.com

For Marty Asher

For my friends who travel in circles

and
in memory of Sam
1988–2003

Womb-of-all, home-of-all, hearse-of-all.
—GERARD MANLEY HOPKINS

We have less time than we knew and that time buoyant,
and cloven, lucent, and missle, and wild.
—ANNIE DILLARD

# CONTENTS

# INTRODUCTION

This book began with a phone call and represents a six-month chronicle of living with cold: where I went looking for winter and the ways in which winter found me. I had been living in a tent on a glacial moraine facing Wyoming's Wind River Mountains for six months. Summer had just ended, and two feet of snow arrived with nighttime temperatures dropping to an unseasonable twelve below zero. When my cell phone rang, I was wrapped in two sleeping bags feeling miserable. It was Marty Asher calling from New York. He asked where I was. I told him. "Perfect," he said, then asked if I would write a book about winter and climate change, about what would happen if we became "deseasoned," if winter disappeared as a result of global warming.

I said I'd think about it. The continental ice caps, glaciers, and frozen seas of the far north where I'd spent so many years loomed in my mind because they were now melting at unprecedented rates. By midcentury, it is predicted, there will be no more glaciers and a million species of living beings will become extinct. The end of winter might mean the end of life. What is the future of winter, of snow, of ice?

Crawling out of my tent, I pulled on knee-high moose-hide boots and sealskin mittens, shoveled through snow to the not-yet-frozen ground, hollowed out a pit, and made a sagebrush fire. As I warmed myself, snow came down, and this chronicle began.

My tent was perched on a rocky knob overlooking a glacier-smoothed meadow backed by crowded peaks that rise to almost fourteen thousand feet. Snow pushed against the nylon walls of the tent, and I pushed back. It was a barren camp, a dry camp, a cold camp, with no running water, no toilet facilities, no trees, no heat. My favorite dog had just died.

I wrote and lived outside, cooked on a Coleman stove, and bathed under the lukewarm stream that came from a solar-heated water bag. On frigid days I used the front seat of my pickup truck for an office, charging my cell phone on the truck battery, thawing frozen food and drying wet clothes on the dashboard. Wolves padded by and antelope grazed the knobs and draws like aliens, their black horns pointing skyward as if listening to something I couldn't hear. A hummingbird visited each day at ten. It circled the tent, flashed its iridescent throat, and left. Mice invaded. I dumped vegetable scraps into badger holes.

Tent life pressed me into what the Tibetans call a mixing of mind and space. By that they mean thought moving with no direction and no bias, yet with a precision capable of taking everything in. The Inuit of Greenland call it *sila*, a word meaning, simultaneously, both weather and consciousness. Living outside for half a year, I began to see how the two are one.

Clouds tickled my ribs and heat waves rippled thought. I

was enveloped by *sabi*—a quiet loneliness that made me laugh. A snowflake came to rest on my eyebrow; I licked a piece of ice snapped from a pond. Weather streamed into my nose, mouth, eyes, ears, and circulated inside my brain.

Weather is all mixed up with movements of mind: a gust can shove one impulse into another; a blizzard erases a line of action; a sandstorm permeates inspiration; rain is a form of sleep. Lightning can make scratch marks on brains; hail gouges out a nesting place, melts, and waters the seed of an idea that can germinate into idiocy, a joke, or genius. How could it be otherwise?

These days seasons no longer come in sequence but are chopped up with heat, storms, blizzards, and droughts. It snowed in June, August, and September and thawed in January and February; record-breaking heat has been followed by record-breaking snow, and the average annual temperature has climbed. This is the signature of a warming climate.

There should be no question about whether global warming is occurring because we now have 450,000 years of climate history at our fingertips provided by the ice cores taken from Greenland and eastern Antarctica, covering the last four glacial and interglacial cycles. We can compare the climate fluctuations before the industrialization of our world and after. We can see clearly how climate has changed.

Ice cores are time machines. Snow piles up, compresses, and becomes firn, then ice mounds up into glaciers; oxygen bubbles are trapped in the ice, providing samples of ancient atmosphere, of how much carbon dioxide and methane is held within. Records of past temperatures and levels of atmospheric gases from before industrialization are compared with those after—a mere 150 years. We can now see that the steady gains in greenhouse gases and air and water temperatures have occurred only since the rise of our nuclear-smokestack-and-tailgate society. The last ten years have seen the most abrupt spikes. Humans have pushed carbon dioxide and methane into the atmosphere at unprecedented levels. Human-caused global warming is overriding that caused by natural fluctuations. Our sky is another kind of tent—not one that shelters but one that kills: it's chock-full of toxins and gases that flow into our bodies and oceans and air and the food we eat. Trapped carbon dioxide is like grief—it has to go somewhere.

We're spoiled because we've been living in an interglacial paradise for twenty thousand years. Now we're losing it. Climate stability, not to mention human superiority and economic viability, are illusions we must give up. Our can-do American optimism and our head-in-the-sand approach to economics when it takes into mind only profit but not the biological health of our planet—has left us one-sided. Too few of us remember how to be heartbroken. Or why we should be. We don't look, because heartbreak might imply failure. But the opposite is true. A broken heart is an open heart, like a flower unfolding from its calyx, the one nourishing the other.

My six-month chronicle took me to both ends of the earth: to the tip of Tierra del Fuego, where I found winter in summer, and to the top of the Spitsbergen (Svalbard) archipelago, where winter was giving way to spring, then returning again.

I followed the orthodromic routes of migrating arctic birds, their great, arcing circles as they flew between Arctic and the icy coasts and islets of the South Atlantic Ocean: arctic terns, long-tailed skuas, jaegers, and sanderlings, among others. But they were on an opposite mission. Instead of looking for winter, they were trying to stay in the warmth and light of summertime, where food was abundant and chicks could hatch, fledge, and fly.

I took up residence in a one-room cabin in Wyoming, wandered snow-embowered valleys on snowshoes and skis, and when water showed itself from under its cover of ice I made a canoe trip down the Green River. In those months winter's hold on me was complete, its grip both a form of concentration and a wide room in which mind and body could roam. I saw the ways in which winter had shaped me, and how our human presence on Earth may well be bringing the season of ice to an end.

What follows is both ode and lament, a wild-time song and elegy, and a cry for help—not for me, but for the tern, the ice cap, the polar bear, and the lenga forest; for the river of weather and the ways it chooses to be born.

# THE FUTURE OF ICE

# PRELUDE:
## A WINTER SOLSTICE BLIZZARD

December 21. Solstice. Why do we talk about sun when there is none? Sol has been banished and snow dissolves night. A wolf howls. The *O* of her mouth is hidden from sight at the edge of the trees. Her voice is echolocation: I'm lost, yet she knows where I am. I traipse to a pine-covered moraine, gulp snow, and go hungry.

In winter I'm both gaunt and voluptuous. I forget food and stumble on flame. At the moment of solstice I try to balance an egg on its end, but it falls, spilling yolk sideways on a pine plank like a broken sun.

It's dark and I walk. I hear movement in the trees; the wolf runs. Willows ringing dry ponds writhe in sudden blasts of snow. On the moraine a pine needle pierces the palm of my hand. I lick sap from a spindly trunk. Wind stops dead. Vanilla brews in the bark of a yellow pine. Far above, in the high peaks, I can hear snow rinsing the wombs of vanished glaciers.


Winter is refuge and deathbed, monastery and ivory tower, cave and ghost. It's where we learn to hiss. In this season we

dive through the Big Dipper's cup to the other side of the con-
stellations; we go behind the scenes of our own lives. As stars
move in their slow adagios, there's a sudden sense of falling
and a blackout union with whatever we stumble upon. Storms
confer powers of concentration; cyclonic winds drive sharp-
shinned snowflakes. The whole world is taken in at once; the
whole world dissolves.


Inside cold there are musical notes: once, while I walked in
hunger and fatigue across the center of northern Greenland's
Warming Land, where no human had ever ventured, rays of
light sprayed out from the ends of my feet. Each time I stepped
down, a burst of music erupted. The earth was a piano and my
feet were searching for chords.

    Here it is dark and I step on light. I climb down to the river
and wander across floating shoals of ice. A dead elk lies draped
over a boulder, her skin gone hard, her black feet piercing ice.
Winter means desiccation, going back to skeleton and bone.
Last week, in the Red Desert, I saw thirsty antelope circling a
frozen pond, pawing to get at water where there was none.


Flesh is ornament, rawhide is real. I wade through powder.
Snow is another kind of air. My footsteps screech. How can
something that comes from cloud feel like plastic? The wolf
drops back into the trees, her mouth clenched tight. Snow has
its own howl—a sixty-decibel silence.

———

Winter is a white vagrancy. There are no days or nights. Just breathing and snow pushing space between thought. I rub my neck. Where lightning drove through me, snow recongeals on neural substrates. By afternoon I feel as if I can touch all the way back to the cells of my brain.

Two ravens stitch a black line between bits of snow. Their love dance, like mine, is a picture of vertigo. The air shakes, then drops and hardens. Snowflakes make dizzying, vaulting leaps. Pine winds bunch needles into whisks for tea, brooms for sweeping away confusion.

Winter is tourniquet: no blood allowed here. From under trees, a white wall curves out like a pouting lip. I can see where a ruffed grouse dove into the snowbank for refuge. Snow is a kind of hard fat. It can nourish and it can kill.

White sky-threads thicken. The moon is out and so is the sun. When they set, darkness rolls at me. I think of Jupiter's brightest moon, Europa, which astronomers say is doodled and freckled, with creamy plains and crypto-icebergs, with a briny sea beneath a mottled ice crust where life might have been or will begin. "I am moved by strange sympathies," Emerson said. The alignment of heart goes only with otherness.

————

At dawn sun beams light-waves in a thousand directions, but as soon as they bounce off some object—bent nail, anthill, snow tire, fly wing—the waves line up, all vibrating in the same direction. So too the creation of consciousness. A streaming wild pulse encounters beings, events, junk heaps, and weather and as a consequence realigns itself into ordered description and memory.

I enter a canyon above two string lakes. On either side pines give gifts other trees do not; their needle whir stirs weather into thought. Snow slides down granite, squalls pulse, each one leading me deeper into the mountains. To put my finger on the end of thought, to stir the heart's beginnings . . . isn't that what life is all about?

After the long storm there is a melting quiet and the hushed roar of wind around high peaks. Long-stemmed aspens click above fallen leaves. There's a descent into a wide valley. The whirl of self vanishes. I sit on a rock and doctor a blister. In that bubble, a whole trapped ecosystem jiggles.

Winter is purgation. It empties us out. Darkness fills the void and snow drains it with light. I look up. White flakes fall past my eyes like tiny pages, each one flashing its redundant narrative. Or is it only ash from the spilled flame and blizzard of solstice?

I stand and walk. Emerson said the first circle is the human eye, but so is the planet. They are linked: the one is always beholding the other.

> *All who come here*
> *feel the lids fall*
> *from their eyes.*
> *This view*
> *of the world without end*
> *there is nowhere to hide.*
> —Muso Soseki

*Part One*

WINTER IN SUMMER

# TIERRA DEL FUEGO

*The straight course is hacked out in rounds
against the will of the world.*

—D. H. LAWRENCE

January. Perpetual freshness, raw cliffs, a leggy forest, an un-polished sun: that's what I've come to love about the end of the world, the uttermost part of the earth, latitude 55 degrees south, last stop before Antarctica. Up under the eaves at the torn end of the Andean cordillera, snow blasts rock walls white and a hanging glacier crumbles. Ocean ends. Ice recedes. Time sweeps upward in the form of southern beech trees; wind rams it back down.

I've come here to hike a seventy-mile circuit in the southern Andes. It's summer but it feels like winter. The trees are bent as if picking up something that had fallen. There is no sunrise, no moonrise, no sighting of the Southern Cross, only storms braiding and unbraiding themselves.

Lately my travels have mimicked the high-altitude circumpolar routes taken by arctic and antarctic birds—south polar skuas, great skuas, long-tailed jaegers, sanderlings, and arctic terns. While we travel the same routes, we are seeking different kinds of weather: they are driven by a tight summer-and-light-seeking schedule ordered by magnetic field lines and sun-compass routes; I'm looking for cold, meandering through wintry landscapes when and where I find them, trying to see if the season of winter is shrinking, and why.

Morning. A single blade of light rays down. I walk the length of the natural harbor below Ushuaia. The town hangs on a hill backed by green peaks. A glut of birds sweeps overhead. Gray-headed albatrosses cross paths with ones that are black-browed, and these pass giant petrels and southern fulmars, as three olivaceaous cormorants flap hard on the water below. Straight south, somewhere between Drake Passage and the South Sandwich Trench, a couple of arctic terns I saw nesting at the very top of Greenland, near Warming Land, have just completed their 107-day trip to these southern waters in search of a twenty-four-hour sun. But here they're getting winter minus the darkness: rain turns to sleet, and in the direction of Cape Horn there is a whiteout of summer snow.

Before me is the historic Beagle Channel, named for the ship that brought young Charles Darwin here, to *el fin del mundo*. It was just before Christmas in 1832 that the HMS *Beagle* turned into the Strait of Le Maire, then the channel. It is a fragment of South Atlantic water into which Drake, Ross,

Cook, Fitzroy, Darwin, Joshua Slocum, and Rockwell Kent, among many others, sailed. They were searching for passage to Asia, looking for gold, or just looking.

This coast was once home to the Yamana Indians, who traveled these rough waters by bark canoe. In the mountains behind Ushuaia lived the Selk'nam (also known as Ona) Indians, guanaco-robed hunters of the harsh Fuegean mountains and plains, whom the Yamana feared.

Today the channel is stippled with whitecaps, the bitterness of vanquished Indians still washing up on its shores. "Is right here everything end," Derek Walcott's Odyssean figure said. What ended was a time when there seemed to be room enough for everyone.

Now the odyssey we human beings in the "developed world" have embarked upon is almost too darkly insane to contemplate. The scandal of "improvement" has meant that we've reduced the parallel worlds of spirit, imagination, and daily life to a single secularized lump. The process of empire building is a kind of denigration. Nothing that's not nuts and bolts and money-making is allowed in.

My toes curl over the edge of the continent dipping into almost freezing water. The westerlies howl. The sea is all slivers and splints, straits and rocky knobs, shinbones and arm bones, hermit islands jutting into desolation bays, as if the history of this place, with its hundreds of shipwrecks and decimated native cultures, were imitating landscape. Or is it the other way around?

"*Kik, kik, kik, kik,*" the terns cry. They will feed and rest here for two months before flying north again. Down here, Argentina and Chile are pinched so tightly together there is almost no land, just peaks, sky strips, and rough water. Evening comes late (it's summer, after all), but a storm-made twilight lasts all day.

Looking out over the famous channel, I think of the tectonic convulsions and hard draughts of heat and ice that have shaped this place and the cold-adapted people who lived here; how beauty in both landscape and culture came from those difficulties. I'm wandering around, trying to connect that which is at the end of the world with the way seasons, ice ages, warm spells, birds, and human thought travel in circles.

Darwin saw Yamana canoes crisscrossing the channel and moving though the labyrinth of inlets and islands. The canoes were built to withstand heavy seas. High-sided, they were made of bark cut from the coihue tree using the long leg bone of the guanaco for a saw, and sewn together with whale sinew strung on whalebone needles.

A canoe lasted for a year. The men were stationed in the bow with harpoons and spears to hunt seals, while the women navigated and paddled. Because it was always cold, the children were placed midboat to tend small fires made from dried grass plants, roots up, stuck into a pile of sand. Smoke was seen coming from every canoe in the channel as well as on every strip of sand.

Rain, wind, or snow was constant, but the Yamana went naked, smearing their bodies with seal and whale grease. They said it was too wet to wear clothes. Their ceremonial dances had the sea in them: the shaman wore a headdress of white bird down meant to look like the foam on a cresting wave. When the people danced, they held sticks horizontally and moved them back and forth, up and down, to represent the movement of the sea.

In the mountains behind Ushuaia, the floor of the valley is bog and peat. Yamana canoe portages were made of felled trees. The logs were laid side by side, sometimes for one thousand feet—a shortcut over soupy ground on which they could carry their canoes or simply walk to distant bays.

Back in the mountains the terrain gets rough and the bogs get deeper. Lakes lie between timbered slopes. The Selk'nam and Haush Indians who lived here hunted their way from one coast to the other. Each time they stopped and built a hut to perform their annual rite, the *kina* ceremony, they said the surface of the ground actually changed: from steep slopes and deep bogs into sunny meadows. It wasn't the spirit doing this, they said, but the ceremony itself that made the earth change.

The Selk'nam had four skies. Each was thought to be invisible and infinite, constituting a whole cordillera. Where they lived was a place of mountains, and they conceived of sky, ocean, and weather as being mountains as well.

The north sky was black, associated with rain, the sea, and the whale. The west was red, made of wind and sun. The east was only a boiling sea, and the south was pure white because that's where the snow came from, and the moon and the owl. These most southerly cultures in the world had winter weather threaded all through them. When asked about who her parents were, one Selk'nam woman said: "I am snow, my mother was wind, my father, rain."

The life of rocks, ice, mountains, snow, oceans, islands, albatross, sooty gulls, whales, seals, crabs, limpets, and guanaco once flowed up into the bodies of these people, and out came whale prayers, condor chants, crab feasts, and guanaco songs. Life went where there was food. Villages were portable. Food occurred in places of great beauty, and the feedback from living directly fueled their movements, dances, thoughts, and lives.

Everything spoke: birds, ghosts, animals, oceans, bogs, rocks, humans, trees, and rivers; everything made a sound, and when they passed one another, a third sound occurred. That's why weather, glaciers, and each passing season were so noisy. Song and dance, sex and gratitude were the season-sensitive ceremonies that linked the human psyche to the larger, wild, weather-ridden world.

When did we begin thinking that weather was something to be rescued from? Why did we trade in our ceremonial lives for the workplace? Is this a natural progression, or a hiccup in human civilization that we'll soon renounce? The *chiexaus* initiation ceremony of the Yamana might last two or three months, and the *hain* initiation ceremony of the Selk'nam sometimes lasted a year, depending on their food supply. In their reckoning, one whale equaled one year.

By the early 1890s vast tracts of Selk'nam and Haush land had been given as land grants by the Argentine government to missionaries as well as land-hungry farmers from the United Kingdom and Europe, who systematically killed, kidnapped, and incarcerated Selk'nam people. One Ona shaman, named Hektliohlh, was detained for years at the Silesean Mission on Dawson Island. When he looked toward his mountain home he said: *"Shouwe t-maten ya,"* the longing is killing me. Then he died. No pure-blood Ona, Yamana, or Haush are left today.

# TORRES DEL PAINE, CHILE

Wild daisies and lenga trees and the winding, milk-green rivers emanating from glaciers. I've been joined by Gary, a friend from Montana, and we are walking. Glaciers have shaped roughly a third of the land area of the planet. How could they not shape the way we move and think, honed as we are, on sharp arêtes, domed cliffs, and the U-shaped valleys between, the floury rivers and string lakes held tight in steep canyons? The southern Andes carry more glacier ice than any other area in the world outside the North and South Poles.

That's why Gary and I are backpacking a seventy-mile circular route in Chile's Torres del Paine National Park. Here the granite batholiths—huge towers—are rock teeth belonging to a wrathful deity from whom perpetual storms spray.

Our backpacks are heavy—mine is fifty-five pounds, and Gary's weighs in at eighty-five. The wind is against us as we head up a steep rise. In my Spanish dictionary the word *senda* means not only "a path," but also "a ways and means," while the masculine, *sendero*, is only "a footpath"—nothing more. Yet the verb, *senderear*, means "to conduct along a path," and also "to attain by tortuous means." Perfect. We follow the

Paine circuit counterclockwise, and as the days go on, I refer to it both as a path that passes with no end in itself and as a circuit of pain. Not just my bodily pain, which at times is considerable, but also the one implied by any circular route consciously taken. Perhaps *circle* is the wrong word. A wheel with broken spokes might be better, or a body following its feet around.


We walk from Hosteria Las Torres, along Río Paine. The sun slides up vertical sweeps and down into U-shaped valleys, giving itself to unraveling storms. The river goes dark, then brightens to a dull celadon. Storm shadows tint tree shadows. Rain shatters and stutters; guanacos graze. Patchworks of ice—the remains of hanging glaciers—rot away before our eyes. Snow squalls fall flat like bedsheets. As we walk through them, they erase both the *sendero* and the *senda*—the path as well as the ways and means. Later, as we go over a pass, an eighty-mile-per-hour wind tips us over. Laughing, we get to our feet and look up: a pair of Andean condors—whose wings, stretched out, are as long as two of me—jump off the cliff above us, a jutting arête, and float effortlessly.

At the end of the first day, before reaching Campamento Serón, we climb onto a flat bench of land, a *mesita* with foot-wide streams and stacked *mogotes*—plants that look like huge pincushions made of yellow flowers growing on hills. A herd of thirty loose horses clatters by on the trail below, pushed by four pantalooned gauchos wearing neck scarves, dark glasses, and berets. The faster the horses go, the more the men laugh. They don't see us; we climb higher. Finally I lay my pack

down, get on my knees, and come face-to-face with a rare
Magellan orchid, its slightly curled petals cream, yellow, and
veined green.

Gary takes off trotting. Lithe and youthful, he jumps
straight-legged from one precipice to another. We met by
chance in the mountains of Wyoming and talked for fifteen
minutes, then didn't see each other again. I dreamt about him.
Same dream each time: he was in a cabin; I walked by outside;
he looked at me with his green eyes. Three months later he
asked a mutual friend for my phone number and called. Another five months went by and many conversations before he
showed up at my door.

My eyes open; Gary is gone, but one, then two, then four condors lift off and soar across the river valley. Their bald heads
and white ermine collars move, but not their wings. Instead,
they let themselves be moved, using their wings, oh so gently,
only to change altitude. To move without effort, that's what I
need to learn. I look up and see a scratched mountain memory:
a glacier's claw mark across a face of rock.

Gary comes back with a condor feather: a gift for me. It is
long and black, its rachis thick and sturdy. Rain comes and
continues all night; I dip the quill into it and write.

The gauchos return for more horses, their laughter rising
and fading as they disappear. We ponder the word *Paine*—for
the circuit we're walking—is it a Telemache word meaning
"blue," or the name of a Welsh climber who scaled a nearby

peak? I know few names here. So many birds, grasses, flowers, mountains, and trees . . .

Sleep comes easily. I'm still tired from traveling and a recent bout of the flu. In the morning I roll the feather in my sleeping pad, hoist my backpack, and reluctantly hit the trail. Oh, for feathers and wings! Effortless is not how I'd describe my movements in the days that follow. Gary and I walk at such different speeds that I see little of him, and for the first time the age difference between us seems appalling. I trudge and saunter, wipe sweat from my face, and laugh at the poorly working parts of my body, while he's all grace and exuberance. Usually an hour ahead, he comes back and carries my pack the last half mile because he's a fair-minded man and is always looking for ways to make our differences equal. At the end of each day we pitch camp, eat soup, drink tea, share chocolate, and happily compare notes: who saw what flower, grass, waterfall, bee, or bird, and how speed or slowness brought these gifts to our eyes.

# UNMARKED

Every day is a circle walked within the big one of the Paine circuit, its outline as unsteady and meandering as our gait. But not as big as the ones the arctic terns, long-tailed skuas, and Baird's sandpipers make. How odd that the northernmost breeding populations of birds are the ones who migrate farthest south.

Once a Chinese Ch'an master asked his head monk where he was going. Fa-yen answered, "I'm rambling aimlessly around." The teacher asked why, and Fa-yen said, "I don't know." The teacher smiled. "That's good."

Farther into the mountains, the river winds in and out and the valleys are white with *romero chilco de magellanes*— wild daisies. As we tramp up a low pass the wind has its way with us and the slopes of stacked-up *mogotes* seem to slide. Below, a river valley of Alaskan proportions opens up: braided oxbows glint and spread wide. To the left of the trail, a waterfall's white crest is hidden, its water seeming to pour directly from clouds. At the center of the circuit the *cerros* are towers of granite whose red shoulders spin like fresh-minted, interior suns pulsing squalls of rain and wind and lobbing heavy-bodied clouds like torpedoes. Here, weather is landscape, and landscape is memory.

We meet four British men on the trail. One of them, Nick Cowles, is a ship's broker who has lived all over the world. He's reeling from the shock of becoming a beast of burden and sleeping on hard ground. Paunchy and gregarious, he's out of shape at only forty-two, but his humor is invincible. He's a novice camper who complains of not sleeping well: "I had to practice lying in a sleeping bag before coming here."

Nick and I ponder the innocence of Darwin as he explored the Andes. Darwin rode horseback over high passes, slept on cold ground, went hungry, suffered illness, saw condors. The impact of his experience on the sea and on the ground was so immense that once he returned to England, he never traveled again and rarely left home.

Gary and I walk and camp, and walk another day. Clouds roil, rain smacks us in the face, snow bends the corners of sharp-edged mountains. We laugh, walking hand in hand, tilting awkwardly in gusts. Down another daisy-filled, steep-sided valley, oxbows break open into circles, and circles widen into lakes—which drain into oxbows again.

The tenth-century Chinese weather predictor Pu-tai wandered aimlessly through the towns of Chekiang. Asked how old he was, he answered, "As old as space." When he slept outside during snowstorms, no snow fell on him.

# LAGO DICKSON

The route we are walking and the way we are walking it reminds me: there are no perfect circles. We're deviants and ec-
centrics, but so is the universe we inhabit, and I'm beginning to
think that's where we've learned our odd ways. In the early
1900s the Yugoslavian mathematician Milutin Milankovitch
updated an old astronomical theory of climate change that
linked the onset of an ice age to the periodic changes in Earth's
orbit around the sun. Precession, obliquity, and eccentricity:
these are what's known as the Milankovitch cycles. Earth is a
blue bulb impaled on a stick wobbling around in the galaxy. It
spins in the universe *en brochette*, and every hundred thousand
years or so, it corrects its orbit to one that resembles a halo. All
this, astronomers say, directly affects our weather, making it
hotter or cooling us down.

The tilt of Earth's axis of rotation is "deranged," they say.
I'd call it being a victim of seduction. The electromagnetic-
field lines shooting from Earth's hot core lure the axial tilt into
aberrant behavior: the straight spine gets bent and the tilt wavers. Ironically, the most deviant behavior—when the rotation

swings most widely—brings on climate stability. Winters might be colder, but the summers are hot, so there's more snow and ice melt and no new ice caps can form.

The smaller the degree of tilt, the more extreme the weather. Winters colder, and summers are mild. High-altitude snow-fields don't melt, and glaciers grow big. "Sounds like politics," Gary complains.

Weather problems start even farther out in space. Earth throws itself at the sun, then makes a hasty retreat. When Earth's orbit around the sun is most constricted, Earth heats up (fewer solar particles to get in the way). But farther out in space, star birth induces the spread of ice, whereas a calm universe sends climate toward warming. Crossing through the spiral arm of a galaxy can stir up cosmic-ray flux, resulting in global cloud cover. Temperatures drop and ice ages begin.

Gary trots ahead and I lag behind. In the distance a two-armed glacier embraces a purple mountain, one white arm on each side. Is the clasp tightening? I wonder. No, it couldn't be. Somewhere in the world, tailpipe emissions are added to the harm from smokestacks, and these swim air and water currents, so that even if we spun though a flux density of volcanic smoke or solar particles, the Earth would only get hotter. A closed circle can be censorious, a dead-ender: trapped greenhouse gases go around and around.

I drain my water jug. Despite my half-assed olfactory powers, I can sense water pushing against a moraine wall a few miles ahead. I'm thirsty, but it will take an hour to get there. Clouds stream over continuously but give no rain. The sky is hard and marbled.

Gary is alternately aloof and passionate, but these days more often aloof. I climb over the split trunk of a lenga tree. Its flesh is the color of cinnamon and burnt orange. So many of my friends have died recently, or are dying, that at times walking this circuit is like being handed from ghost to ghost. Dying is a way of completing a circle. I'm hungry; I'm climbing over bodies; I walk on.


Somewhere along the trail, utterly tired, I stop to lay my pack down and pull out the map. Nothing on it makes sense. Perhaps it is a guide for the perplexed and will lead me somewhere new. Maybe not. I look up. A broken branch, old and mossy, has hung its forked arms around the living trunk of a young tree. The trunk squeaks as it grinds against the aging arms of its lover. Tree love. An arboreal song.

Condors leap from cliffs. They're not suicidal, merely going to visit another mountain range. When a condor jumps and flaps its wings, the pressurized air slams against the mountains, wiping mist off, pushing a boat-shaped shadow over our heads. Every brush of a wing has repercussions. A piece of ice calves, a bow wave pulls across a lake; a stone is turned and a river changes course; a dust mote rises into a cloud and comes down as snow; a tree dies and the global climate changes.

———

It's a lip of dirt and rock, and we're climbing it. On the other side is the anticipated lake. We skid down a steep trail, take off our boots and jackets at the bottom, and lie prostrate in the sun. Laughter wakes us. It's the Brits. One of them is diabetic and the others are joking about the proper procedure if he goes into a coma. "Do we give the shot in his ass or his arm? Do we put a pill under his tongue? And which pill?" The more savage the teasing, the louder the laughter. They are school chums who have known one another most of their lives. For the first time the winds have stopped and the sun is shining. Jokes about mortality fly through the air. Our own and the planet's. I smile without bothering to open my eyes. It's like dying, this healing warmth, this laughter.

## NIVEL DEL BOSQUE

Are we the needle carrying a thread around a circle? We nose through *el bosque magellenico*—a mixed forest of coigue, lenga, and nirre. In a dark valley we come on *carpinterías*—woodpeckers with red heads and black wing feathers—one on every tree. The canopy throws green sun on us, then green mist and green rain. Looking up I see parts of broken tree branches hanging: a cross, a pair of legs, a torso. Are these the dead and disappeared of Argentina, the bodies of dead friends?

Tree line wavers. As ice melts and temperatures rise, the limits of tree growth on a mountain expand. Trees move upward in warm times and down when the earth cools. Scientists are trying to register the tiny shifts in the niches of plants, insects, animals, trees, fish, water, and soil caused by the spikes and jolts in the weather we are now experiencing.

Rain falls. We eat sausage and bread in a tin shed built for *mochilleros*—backpackers—to get out of the weather. The camp looks like a hideout for vigilantes—dank, cold, eerie. A gaucho wearing sheepskin chaps with the wool still on is unpacking a horse. Just beyond, in bold sunlight, Río Los Perros roars. Gary asks why it's called "Los Perros" but gets a shrug. I look up and down the river but there are no dogs. Instead, four ducks stand facing the oncoming current, opening their mouths to let food come in. We cross the river on a half-rotted swinging bridge. Just because we're walking in a circle doesn't mean the path isn't provisional. Anyway, *circle* isn't quite the right word. The path is what is passing under our feet and in our minds. It takes us around.

As we reenter the forest, a green cloud spoils our view. Water opens the way. I breathe deeply as the trail moves to the edge of the river. Just below the light and roar and *whoosh* of a waterfall there's a midstream island where we camp, squatting in frigid water to bathe, building a small fire to warm ourselves. Eating soup, we sleep in the water-arm embrace of white noise.

# PANTANO

It is a fresh wound, a whole shoulder torn, with a watery ooze and a hole that's getting bigger. I'm walking through a hanging bog, one that is cupped by the upper reaches of a mountain. Stunted trees bend sideways like dislocated hands. As I walk, I see how the wound grows, where backpackers have climbed farther up to avoid the mud but, in so doing, have torn the Earth's skin more.

How fragile we are. We being humans and this mountain. The sun is gone and snow clouds pour in. The trees thin. Gary has sprinted ahead and disappeared, and it's hard to guess which of many trails he's taken. I choose one and enter the wound, trying not to get my feet wet because snow clouds are gathering and surely it will freeze by evening. My foot is a knife, tormenting the mountain's body.

A lone hiker comes from the other direction looking haggard, his leggings torn, boots muddy, with a trail of blood down his neck where his earring was snagged and torn. Is it wet up ahead? he asks. No, it's an easy forest walk to Lago Dickson.

He thanks me. Sydney? I ask. "No, Perth." Ah, the home of the writer Tim Winton! "Yes, it is," he says, smiling brightly, and continues downhill. I go the opposite way, though for a moment I want to join him.

Bog walking is like these mountain conversations: it means jumping fast and running over uncertain ground. But my pack is heavy, I'm tired, and the spring has gone from my step. I hop, sink, pull my leg out, tip sideways, hop again. One misstep and my boot sinks deep. Soupy mud pours in around my feet. In the muck I see flecks of ice as if whole winters have been lost here.

Yet my sense of this place is of a shoulder that's inflamed. Rain and snow may fill it, trying to put out the fire, but there is no balm. The word *pantano* means not only "bog" but also "impediment." I think of the ones between Gary and me and trip on tree roots buried in brown taffy. The coming storm makes me worry about hypothermia, wet feet and boots. I continue up alone. *Es muy borrascoso*—stormy. Am I lost? The ground steams. The stunted trees are bent completely over. I step on a path. It leads me out of the bog onto dry ground.

# THE PASS

The way is rock-strewn and bare with tarns the size of foot-baths. I wipe daubs of mud from arms and face, grinning because I'm in open country. To be above tree line is to be completely alive. A speck moves at the top of a ridge. It's Gary, glissading down the face of the mountain. A few minutes later he appears from behind an outcrop, exuberant: "That was fun! I think I'll do it again, okay?" He trots straight up and glissades down. Far above, snow-filled valleys nest between hanging glaciers, and waterfalls thread past the curved lips of lateral moraines. When he reappears, we join hands and continue on.

Walking switchbacks is like rising in an elevator: green walls fall away and the mountaintop comes into view. Here there are none of the easy graces of summer. No greenery, no cornucopia of flowers and food. The only inflorescence is rock, the way it turns in a stream and flicks light.

Everywhere I see how glaciers have shaped this place: rock walls carry the signatures of moving ice. These glaciers are remnants of the last ice age. In two and a half million years the earth has been gripped by glaciers and continental ice sheets at least fifteen times. Glaciers have sculpted roughly one third of the earth's landmass. During ice ages, birds, fish, plants, trees, and mammals were pushed toward the equator. What's left behind are new surfaces: kettle moraines, outwash plains, pingos, and scoured barren grounds. Ice scrapes the earth as if it had claws. Look closely: this is all that is left of the world's body after ice has picked the bones clean.

The mountain pass we are supposed to cross looks close but is a few hours' walk straight up. On the way a serac falls and the waist of a glacier—a series of accumulation crevasses—crumbles. The rhythm of glaciers is not something we can hear. It is an ancient memory of sound carved in long grooves and nervous chatter marks, thundering erratics bouncing on the undermelody of shushing streams of ice. Glaciers represent what is bold, inscrutable, exposed, quiet, and glinting in us, as well as what is delicate, dynamic, and precise. If we walk among them long enough, perhaps we can learn from them.

We walk on rubble. Spires are wind-sharpened. We look up at glaciers while walking on the dents and scuff marks that ice has left behind; we walk on its walking. Traversing the spine, we reenter the womb and climb into the cranium, where mist pivots. The sky borrows from ice its radiance, its adamantine clarity, and we spend lifetimes tracking down those elements within ourselves. Moving single-file, Gary and I are reptilian—one undulating organism. Behind us the green-tailed, tree-covered cordillera falls away like sorrow.

# ICEBERGS

Gary tries to take a picture of the two of us, sitting on top of a moraine wall, looking down at a meltwater lake strewn with icebergs, but his attempts fail. "I've got to go down there," he says finally, meaning the lake. "I've never seen an iceberg." He runs down the steep side of the bowl. At the bottom he slides, half stumbling, then jumps a patch of water onto a berg. Crouching, he's pensive, studying cracks, the half-hidden explosions of turquoise, the glacial till embedded in ice. On his hands and knees, he wipes meltwater on his face and gauges a glacier's brightness by holding a piece of ice to his eye. He's looking at time and impermanence, how each snowflake may be trapped for three hundred years, compressed as ice, and put in service to the body of a glacier before being released at the terminus; he sees how a glacier grows by giving away almost as much as it has received. Accumulation and ablation, to get and to give: these are the balancing acts of any human or glacier.

———

A waterfall peels out of a cave, rounding the granite lip over which it has traveled for thousands of years. Everything we need to know about beauty, justice, time, movement, subtlety, and surrender is here. Ideas implicit in nature but difficult for us humans to enact in our own lives.

We climb and climb. Hoarse-throated streams rush past. No scent of humans and horses, only the tang of snow. A single flower sheltered by an overhanging rock shivers.

Late in the day we make camp five hundred yards below the pass on a flat surrounded by krummholz—stunted trees to which we tie the tent in a hard wind. I gather twigs and make a fire. We finish our nightly meal of soup in spitting snow that quickly becomes a blizzard. Night comes as a white monstrosity. Shadow asks the body, are you there?

Snow taps the tent. Down the long valley, *la falda*—the green skirt of trees—is dusted white. What we see of the world is only the mind's invention, Philip Whalen, the poet, said. Once, during a bad spell after a miscarriage while cowboying, I slept on the raked gravel of a friend's New Mexico courtyard. The rough texture consoled me and mirrored the way I felt after losing the child.

Now we sleep on a barren womb that was once filled with ice. I have no children, and I'm with a man who wants them. Isn't all this beauty enough? I ask. Do we need more? When I go out to pee I step on snowflakes, each one a singular geometry, what Frank Lloyd Wright called "the grammar and spell-power of form."

Gary lays the black condor feather by my sleeping bag and takes off his clothes. He seems weightless, not thin, but slim-waisted, with narrow legs that move like wings. He is under me, beside me, over me, then under again. Wet snow slaps at the tent. A zipped door flutters. The feather lifts and we go with it—all the hesitations between us lightened. Wind rattles stays and nylon. Snow plasters the roof and sides. We slide into a pulsing darkness—not a fearful place but a room of winter where we are quiet, lost inside each other for a long time.

Later I peek out; there's been a break in the storm. Across the valley I see a scooped-out shelf where there was once a hanging glacier. Now it's an empty bowl. Lit by moonlight, it chimes.

Voices and laughter wake us. It's already noon. Last night's wind carried the half-moon in a cloud basket. Now it rides out of the sky on a condor's wings. The Brits pad up the trail below our tent, where Gary and I are having an argument about whether it's my birthday. We can come to no conclusion. There's always a blizzard on my birthday, I say. But we don't know what day it is, he replies. I snort. That doesn't mean it's not my birthday, I tell him. The Brits disappear as we break camp. Carefully, I roll my condor feather inside my sleeping pad and tie it onto my pack, hoping it will wing me upslope from behind.

The pass is a wind-hardened saddle so wide and bare it's like looking over the edge of the earth. We start down, then see something white—maybe it's the meteor that fell into the inland ice sheet of Greenland a few years ago and was never seen again. But it's not. It's a low-riding, slow-moving glacier with a six-mile-wide roof, called Ventisquero Grey.

We sit down, stunned. Its white hulk has no beginning or end. Blue-blasted crevasses and fluted channels fill our eyes. "Is it the moon rising?" Gary asks. No, it's the moon going down, I say. A midglacier ice stream softens into a smooth valley, its sides all ruffles. Blue leaves peel. Pinnacles of ice are top hats carrying debris, hauling turquoise down to a distant lake, whose blue milk we will drink in our tea.

# DESCANSO

"Be your own lamp, your own refuge," the Buddha said as he was dying. Same thing my Tibetan teacher told me before he passed on. But I'm lost; I'm dropping straight down. For a moment I see the glacier's white flank flashing, then it disappears. Hours before, Gary raced down into thick trees. It is a tangled labyrinth on a vertical slope with a footing of greasy mud that does not hold me. Sometimes the trees are marked with orange paint, but there is no trail. I bend under contorted branches and let myself down by hanging from a tree branch, then dropping two or three feet to the next foothold. The weight of the fifty-five-pound backpack punishes my knees. I slip, fall, and crack my shin against an exposed root. In a sudden fury, I take my pack off and throw it down as far as I can. The pack slides in the mud and bumps to a stop against a tree. I retrieve it and continue down. Eight hours later I've "mastered" something like 3.5 miles.

Why do we walk around and around, bodies hurting, every broken bone feeling as if it is breaking again? Gary suggests that a new translation of the Buddha's words about "being your own lamp" might urge us to install solar power in transcontinental circuits, lighting the big cities and the small.

On a ridge above the trees where I think I see mountains there is only scalloped fog, and my shadow moving across it, a lone figure bent under a too-heavy load. At the bottom I find other hikers, including the Brits, a couple from Germany, and a threesome from the French Alps, all huddled under a shed. It's raining again. I'm finding it hard to walk. We joke about installing a knee surgeon here.

# THE BATH, THE RIVER, THE WALL

A half-moon hangs in the sky at midday. For the first time, the wind is pushing us from behind. We climb out of forest gloom and treachery onto a rocky ridge and make camp overlooking the glacier's crumbling terminus. At sunset, other trekkers join us. We watch pinks and purples drain off the top of the ice and pool in meltwater lakes on the glacier's roof, "like pink gin," Nick says.

Gary goes into the forest to find a place to bathe. I find him crouched behind two enormous logs. A stream trickles down a staircase of rock and feeds into a shadowy pool. The leaves are dripping onto him.

He stands in a wide plié, then shifts his weight to one knee. His hair is wet. I take off my clothes and squat down at water's edge. Moss is our only washcloth. We are hidden and naked; we lower our bodies into cold leaf-broth. A soft rain falls down.

In the morning a roaring mountain stream brings us to a vertical rock wall. Wind gusts hard at seventy miles an hour. We climb the face on a rickety ladder made of cut tree limbs and cable. Nose to the wall, I meet a dull mirror of basalt. Who's there? An imposter. Everything about my life seems foolish and fraudulent. Wind kicks me in the ass. The backpack shifts sideways. Hope I don't fall.

Halfway up I think of the things I'd like to do before I die: live for a year with binocular vision, speak only animal languages, start sleepwalking again, and do away with all automobiles. I grab rung after rung and pull myself up. In Japan I met Yamabushi, ascetic mountain monks who climb ladders made of knife blades and are hung upside down by their heels in frigid waterfalls. Mountains invite us to humiliate ourselves. They bring danger and difficulty, and drive beauty to the bone.

From atop the tree-branch ladder, a waterfall's icy cascade is winter-in-summer sliding down. I wash my face. Bad dreams from the night before still hang on. Dreams not about the Earth coming to an end but about my own demise. I was hiding from soldiers in a high cupboard in my childhood bedroom; I'd been discovered there and taken away. The dream woke me. I flung a desperate arm over Gary's back and wondered if I'd ever be able to sleep alone again.

# LAGO GREY

To our dismay, we find we've entered civilization. We pitch our tent at the only place possible—in a designated campground at Lago Grey. It's noisy and crowded but cheerfully so. There are Australian, Argentine, French, German, Iranian, Chilean, and British backpackers on the circuit, as well as day tourists brought in by boat from the other shore. At the kiosk Gary and I buy a small box of local wine, sit in the sun with our backs against a rock wall, and let the alcohol have its way.

The lake is raw silk, blue-gray with slubs of ice threaded through. "Or nubs," Gary says. "Or maybe toes." He's smiling. Mountains pierce space; space pierces the mountains. "The kind you fall through?" Gary asks. "The kind you are made from," I say. The party boat chugs across the lake toward us, lands, and takes all but the backpackers away.

The snout of the glacier changes from blue to gray. Above, there are other mountains with glaciers like white scarves pulled around their necks. Lake water slaps black gravel at our feet. What we are seeing here is either a lake in the making or a glacier on the make, but because we've temporarily lost our power of discernment, we can't tell.

In the morning Gary fashions a walking stick for me to ease the weight on my knees. I hoist my pack on, dig in. Every time I take a step my knees lock up, and for the first few yards I have to hit the backs of my legs to get them moving. Absurd as I am, I keep going. I think of the short staffs carried by Zen monks during ceremonies, meant to represent an upturned tree. Roots up, they signify strength, discipline, and impermanence. I imagine this whole forest torn out, the trees upended, their roots flailing at the sky.

# THE BUMBLEBEE

Raindrops, sun, a single cloud wheeling between two condors. Why do we walk in circles? The birds circle nothing, their flight pattern describing the mathematical theory of zero, an open mouth from which *la bufera*—perpetual storm—falls. We take a side route that goes up to interior peaks. It's an easy walk, a low traverse around the edge of the mountains. A young gaucho races toward me on a gray horse and excitedly tells me that a hiker broke his leg and he's going to get help. *Bueno, adiós,* I say. Not long afterward, he returns, leading another horse back up the mountain. Soldiers troop by, with the injured man, his leg in a splint, riding the palomino. I ask if he needs pain pills. He grins. "I've had plenty, thank you," he says.

It rains again. We make camp quickly and take to the tent. River sounds push Gary into sleep, and I listen to *sila*—how the mind-litter roils with chaotic weather. We are made of weather and our thoughts stream from the braid work of still- ness and storms. For years Nietzsche searched for what he called "true climate," for its exact geographical location as it corresponds to the inner climate of the thinker. He might as well have gone searching for the ever-drifting North Pole. It would have been fitting—because the tip of Earth's axis of rotation wobbles like a spinning top, the peregrinations of the North Pole describe a circle.

Río Frances roars by. When the rain stops I wash our shirts and socks and hang them on a line between two trees. After sausage and crackers, Gary goes his way, and I hike up the mountain and sit in a pile of boulders overlooking the river. There's a glacier tucked up in a cirque, and its edges are ragged. The trim line of lenga trees is clearly visible: leggy roots hang over the cliff carved away by ice, as if surgery has just been performed.

A collar of ice encircles the glacier's top edge, not white but eggshell blue. Twenty thousand years ago temperatures plummeted and ice grew down from the top of the world in long vines and wide groundcovers. Glaciers sprouted and surged, covering 10 million square miles—more than thirteen times what they cover now. In the southern Andes, ice sheets fingered their way between high peaks all the way south to the Strait of Magellan and the Beagle Channel.

Now clouds slide over, banking up, one on top of the other, as if trying to help the glacier grow. But this one is receding. Already its forehead has been torn open and is poised to fall.

Worldwide, glaciers are on the wane. As a result, the albedo effect—the ability of ice and snow to deflect heat back into space—is declining as glaciers melt and less and less snow covers the ground each winter. Snow and ice are the Earth's built-in air conditioner, crucial to the health of the planet. Without winter's white mantle, earth will become a heat sponge, and only smoke from a volcano could shield us from incoming UV rays. As heat escalates, all our sources of fresh water—already in danger of being depleted—will disappear.

The warming Earth is causing meltwater to stream into oceans, changing temperature and salinity; sea ice and permafrost is thawing, pulsing methane into the air. Seawater is expanding, causing floods and deep intrusions into rivers and estuaries; islands are disappearing, and vast human populations in places like Bangladesh are in grave danger. The high-mountain peoples of Peru, Chile, and Bolivia who depend on meltwater from snowpack are at risk of being lost; the Inuits of Siberia, Alaska, arctic Canada, and Greenland who depend on ice for transportation and live on a diet of marine mammals will disappear. The early onset of spring and the late arrival of winter is creating ecosystem pandemonium in temperate climates everywhere.

It is not unreasonable to think that a whole season can become extinct, at least for a time. Winter might last only one day—minor punctuation in a long sentence of heat. Mirages rising from shimmering heat waves would be the only storms.

We have already destroyed so much natural vegetation on the planet that the increased heat due to bare ground, ineffectual rainfall, and city pavement will have particularly dire effects with nothing to modify them. Land-ocean-atmosphere-solar-galactic cycles are inextricably linked. One flap of the butterfly and everyone fries.

———

A hem is torn out. Clouds unzip and drop rain. An ice block falls, thundering down between the bare walls of the couloir. A stream of water erupts, baring a rock wall. This is how a river grows longer in high mountains: by going uphill. Let me explain. As the glacier recedes, the waterline—the point at which water begins to flow—shifts upward. Perhaps this glacial river will someday meet its source: the snowflake that fell one thousand years ago.

Gary returns from a six-hour walkabout. We argue about how long our "short-term" relationship can possibly last. A snow squall migrates down the narrow canyon toward our tent. I grab the shirts and underwear I washed and pull them in. The wrathful and peaceful deities at the center of this mountain complex are still spinning storms around with their hundred flailing arms, still telling us what, in Sanskrit, is called a *pariplava*—a circular story. Things between us will end when they end. But not yet. There are more storms to come. Behind clouds, sun strobes. If the path is whatever passes, no end in itself, why are we walking in a circle? Why don't we just stand?

For a minute the clouds clear and the orange granite towers peek through. A single bumblebee flies by our tent, headed into the storm. In the high Arctic at latitude 80 degrees north the *Bombus polaris* shiver to keep warm. The worker bees die at the end of summer, and the impregnated queen starts a new colony when warm weather returns. I don't know this bee, but it must be cold-adapted in ways that we humans are not. Will it be able to adapt to heat? Gary and I hold each other; we shiver with cold. The bee is bright orange and looks like a piece of fire.

# PERITO MORENO: CHRONICLES OF ICE

A trapped turbulence. As if wind had solidified. Then noise: timpani and a hard crack, the glacier's internal heat spilling out as an ice stream far below. I've come on a bus from El Calafate to see this World Heritage glacier.

Some glaciers retreat, some surge, some do both, advancing and retreating even as the climate warms. The surface of Perito Moreno is 160 square miles across. It advances six feet per day at the center. From the platform where I'm standing, I can look directly down on the glacier's snout. Two spires tilt forward, their tips touching. They meet head-to-head, but their bodies are hollow. Sun scours them; they twist toward light.

Gary is gone. He has taken the bus to Río Gallegos and from there will continue north. He wanted to walk two more routes; he wanted to be alone. I watched the bus back slowly out of the station and disappear down a hill. Afterward, I caught a ride to this face of ice to see its bowls, lips, wombs, fenders, gravelly elbows, ponds, and ice streams, and to learn whatever lessons a glacier might teach me.

———

A glacier is not static. Snow falls, accretes, and settles, until finally its own weight presses it down. The flakes become deformed: they lose coherence and pattern, become firn that turns to ice. As an ice mountain grows, its weight displaces its bulk and it spreads outward, filling whole valleys, hanging off mountains, running toward seas.

There are warm glaciers and cold glaciers, depending on latitude and altitude. Warm glaciers have internal melt-streams at every level and torrents of water flow out from under the ice at the glacier's toe. The "sole" of the glacier is close to the melting point and slides easily over rock. The quasi-liquid surface that results forms a disordered layer, a complicated boundary where heat and cold, melting and freezing, play off each other and are inextricably bound, like madness and sanity, silence and screams.

Friction creates heat; heat increases sole melt, slipperiness, and speed. Because ice melts as it moves and moves as it melts, a glacier is always undermining itself; it lives by giving itself away.

Cold glaciers don't slide easily; they're fixed and frozen to rock. They move like men on stilts: all awkwardness on broken bones of sheared rock. Internal deformation affects flow patterns: melting occurs faster at the margins than in the center. A glacier's velocity is parabolic, its internal melt-streams deep and swift yet sinuous. Their meandering is said to be regular and precise, like a mind going for a walk.

A glacier balances its gains and losses like a banker. Accumulation has to exceed ablation for it to grow. At the top, snow stacks up and does not melt. Midway down, the area of "mass balance" is where the profits and losses of snow can go either way. Surface melting can mean that water percolates down, refreezes, melts, and freezes again, creating a lens of ice, a Cyclopean eye. Unlike the dry powder at top, this is the wet snow zone, where profits melt but losses can be regained quickly.

Below this region of equilibrium, ablation occurs. Profits are lost there when the rate of melting exceeds the rate of accumulation. But a glacier can still advance if enough snow falls at the top and stays.

Everything is always becoming something else. But glacier ice goes only one way: toward more ice, or ice that is becoming water—because ice never reverts directly back to being a snowflake. In Japan's snow country, people say that ice and water are yin—female—and snow is yang—male; that a glacier starts out masculine but quickly becomes a moving giant of femininity.

Ice comes from water but can teach water about cold, the poet Muso Soseki says. After, it goes back to being water again. A glacier's fenders and underpinnings can move at different speeds, yet it appears to be a single mass. In midsummer crevasses deepen and meltwater ponds can split open. The fissures cut straight down, and the turquoise eyes drain. This is water teaching ice how to become water.

———

A glacier is a kind of blind eye. It can hoard snow without seeing how big its own body is getting. And it can give away more than it takes in. Is this compassion or self-loathing? What makes it act this way? For a glacier, the first law of impermanence is: something has to give.

A glacier is an archivist and historian. It saves everything no matter how small or big, including pollen, dust, heavy metals, bugs, bones, and minerals. It registers every fluctuation of weather. A glacier is time incarnate, a moving image of time. When we lose a glacier—and we are losing most of them—we lose history, an eye into the past; we lose stories of how living beings evolved, how weather vacillated, why plants and animals died. The retreat and disappearance of glaciers—there are only 160,000 left—means we're burning libraries and damaging the planet, possibly beyond repair. Bit by bit, glacier by glacier, rib by rib, we're living the Fall.

I walk down stairs to a platform that gives me a more intimate view of the glacier's face. A row of ice teeth is bent sideways, indicating basal movement. Out of the corner of my eye something falls. A spectator gasps. An icy cheekbone crumbles. People become enthralled by the falling and failings, forgetting about the power it takes for the glacier to stay unified.

From inside the glacier there's a deep rumbling. Internal

warfare, someone says. In some places the ice has warmed enough to undulate, as if trying to make itself look like open sea, its roof, all crenulations, a whole ocean of ice. Other, smaller glaciers ride distant mountains to join the mass. Right here, a snow squall dissipates and sun touches our shoulders. Thunder emanates from behind a million blue spires. So much in a glacier, like so much in a brain, is hidden, we don't know what a thought or a mass of ice is saying, or why it moves.

A sign tells me that an internal stream is running at a depth of 180 meters and is called the Canal de los Tempanos. More drums sound. Water pours from the portal at the glacier's foot. Sun shines. White whiskers snap. A piece of wall breaks and drops, and waves radiate out carrying the shards. For now the glacier advances and almost nothing is lost: all the broken bones are subsumed by the ice's hungry foot. Or are they?

The wind shifts; bits of ice curl back on water and are shunted into a cove. Up top, the snow squall advances; below, an azure turret tears away, revealing what looks like a ruptured spleen. No blood, only turquoise glistening.

I walk to a different level. A blue dome made of bent spires collapses into itself. Ice falls down the front of the portal, starting a riptide, causing the river to swallow itself. Timpani sounds. Or is it a hammer tapping glass? A gunshot? A whole leaf of ice spills forward. What is the final straw that makes ice break?

A moment, that's all it will take in geological time, for the sun to torch this glacier. I start climbing stairs. There are a thousand of them—same as the height of the ice. *"Andale,"* the bus driver calls out. It's 9:00 p.m. but still light, and I don't want to leave. Can it be that human and animal life and the life of this glacier are coming to an end all because we didn't care enough to stop their destruction?

The sun starts to drop and the ice goes purple. Life ends like this every night and revs up again in the morning. Climbing the stairs is like climbing a waterfall, the violet foliage of ice melting and rushing over my feet. It is dark and the current of the vertical lays me flat. The Milky Way comes into being, and pours virtual water on real Patagonian dust.

The bus takes me back to town. I get out near a grove of trees where saddle horses have been let loose to wander. It's good to be in a place where there are such freedoms.

At the edge of a half-dry lake I look toward mountains. Gary's sudden absence currents through me. Love without attachment—is it possible? "Loneliness is the starvation of ego," Trungpa Rinpoche said. Around the lake's cracked mirror four birds begin to sing. Evensong, or else the blues. All that's holding me together at the moment is the thought of the terns in the middle of their molt. Some are sitting on bits of ice drifting south; others are in the water eating krill. Discarded flight feathers bump across the chop. The birds wait. Wind grooves the Weddell Sea; new flight feathers are growing.

I eat alone at a rustic bar with other travelers. It's late when night comes, maybe ten-thirty. Gary is traveling north into hot, dry mountains. I'll take winter anytime. "Why pretend to light an empty lantern?" an old Chinese proverb goes. In the darkness, Perito Moreno is still calving and moving, grabbing snowflakes, stirring weather, spitting out ice water, and it makes me smile.

# SWIMMING STRAIGHT,
# WALKING IN CIRCLES

Arctic terns know that the return is different from the beginning. They flew eleven thousand miles in August from an island off central Greenland, down the coast of Europe to South Africa, then used the south polar winds to take them to Antarctica. But to return they'll follow the coast of Patagonia, turning east at Cabo São Roque in Brazil, then fly north with the Gulf Stream.

Flying out of El Calafate, I return alone to Ushuaia and check into the same hotel. Guillermo gives me a room on the back side, facing the patio, where he's working on the mast of the boat that brought him here from Buenos Aires. "But now I won't be sailing very far," he tells me. "This is my home; my girlfriend owns this hotel."

I lie on the bed and close my eyes. When I was a child I'd pretend that the silverware at the dinner table was very heavy, and struggle to lift a fork or spoon. My charade brought laughter. Now I wonder why I feel so light. Why the terns' contrails of sinew, feather, and bone are the only things carrying me.

To a friend at a Zen center, I email that I feel disoriented. He replies immediately: "Disoriented from WHAT?" I buy a bottle of wine and drink it. The local newspaper carries a story about a Patagonian toothfish that made a transequatorial migration all the way to Greenland. While Gary and I were hiking the Paine circuit, this fish was swimming in a straight line. The toothfish, whose home is the ocean off the Antarctic, weighed 154 pounds. Also known as a Chilean sea bass, although it is not a true bass, it is endangered from overfishing. The farthest north such a fish has ever been found is off the coast of Uruguay. This one swam from latitude 45 degrees south to latitude 63 degrees north. It could only have made the trip by diving deep and using the cold currents that run beneath the tropical ones at the equator.

The toothfish was caught by a fisherman in Davis Strait off the west coast of Greenland. Where was it going? Was it swimming laps between the poles? The fish must have been hungry when it died. When the fisherman opened it up, the only thing in its stomach was the upper beak of a cephalopod.

I lie back on the bed. The arctic tern, with its lightweight, hollow wing bones, logs in something like 600,000 miles during its twenty-five-year life. The hippocampus of any migratory bird is said to be larger than one in a bird that stays put. For the bird on the wing, memory needs to tackle more, so the brain enlarges to accommodate increased input. Perhaps the same is true for fish and even humans. If so, I'm in luck. I haven't spent more than three months in any one place for years.

Right now I'm tired of vagrancy. Maybe I should change my mode of travel. I want to travel meridians, not latitudes, and trace a magnetic line from stem to stern. I want to feel how the force of the Earth's rotation churns the flow of ocean nutrients and pushes warm surface water westward away from its shore. I want to slice through current flows, through regions of water that have never mixed, and take the pulse of a storm by placing my three fingers on its wrist. I want to drink ocean weather instead of wine and dance to the brain's metronome of transient electrochemical throbs.

I want to follow a male tern during courtship as he catches a fish in his mouth and offers it to his loved one, waiting to see if she will take that prize. I want to fly wingtip to wingtip with long-tailed skuas, sanderlings, terns, and jaegers until the dead-end, austral shore of antarctic ice comes into view. Then, in February, begin the terns' long flight north, arriving in May at the old nest site on Oodaaq Island, latitude 83 degrees north in Greenland.

If I can't do that, I'll think of other things: I'll build a hut on the Barren Grounds. Writing will happen only at night. I'll sleep only in direct sun. I'll swim naked under the ice. I'll ride the back of the toothfish all the way home.

We humans with our blunted senses know so little about things. What does the toothfish know, or the tern? Even our own bodies are mysterious to us. I read that human male sperm has a sense of smell and swims directly toward the ovum once it catches the scent. I want to sniff that deep perfume. Not the season but the seasoning—that's what I want. And the man with the sperm.

Recently I've had trouble telling when any season actually begins, since it snowed on the vernal equinox and the autumnal equinox as well as on the winter and summer solstices. That's how I know our confusion is semantic—it isn't the season that matters but the deeper forces at work: the way an ooze of water tears at the ground, widening a way to become a river. I want geological violence speeded up so I can see it. I want winter in the form of white swans.

The next morning Guillermo suggests that I go down to the dock and hitch a ride on a boat cruising the Beagle Channel. We sail out in calm seas and my eyes fill: Magellanic penguins cling to a rocky islet and face the sun with open mouths, closed eyes. While they sleep, seals cavort. A black-browed albatross cruises by the hulking remains of a wrecked ship.

Tucked up into the cirques of these coastal mountains are the remnants of glaciers that Darwin described as covering almost the whole mountain. Now ice has receded and tree line struggles upslope. We visit Harberton, the historic sheep ranch where, as a young man, Lucas Bridges "went native" and became an initiate of the Yamana and Selk'nam tribes.

To the south are rocky islets, stepping-stones through the furious seas that lead to the Larsen Ice Shelf of Antarctica. Terns are aloft, but so far up I can't tell if they are *Sterna paradisaea* or common terns that live in Tierra del Fuego year round.

At the end of the day the boat heads home. Far ahead, the entire Darwin Range has been blasted white. Just a summer snowstorm, a German geographer says. The weather turns cold and blustery. A young Argentine woman stirs up a tiny pot of maté and offers it to us. We take turns sipping tea from a silver straw while the sun goes down. I read aloud from *Voyaging*, written by Rockwell Kent when he sailed this way in the 1920s, stopping to paint and explore: "We drop away, the widening black water tosses up the ship's reflected lights like flames," he wrote. "We pass out of the illuminated radius into the darkness, and by the darkness into the solitude of the world's end."

*Part Two*

# THE WHITE DAY

*Life: an intermittent fever between long lapses of quiet.*

—ROBERTO CALASSO

*2*

February. A whale, an owl, a grebe. There's a new moon, the tiniest sliver, its belly-weighted shadow pushing that one edge into light. Below is an estuary full of bellowing frogs and an ocean of unturned waves. A heron balances on a mat of kelp. A dolphin leaps straight up out of the water, a silvery, wiggling mass of joy. Sometimes it's hard to remember what a mess we're making of our planet. The sea exhales; mist wafts over cool sand.

I walk the beach in California. At waterline, a Chumash spear point tumbles at my feet, spins like a compass, and points north. I pack my winter things—parkas, snowshoes, cross-country skis, and moose-hide packs, plus Gaby, my dog, and begin driving.

Now hot, now cold, rain curing to snow and back to rain, hail bulleting sand. It's not always so that winter comes on schedule, that flakes fall straight down and stay. I've been driving and driving: east to the Mojave Desert, north to Mount Whitney, northeast into Nevada's Jarbidge Wilderness, north through Idaho to Glacier National Park.

Oh how funny it is: that I'm to write about winter and can't find it. As soon as I arrive somewhere the dusting of snow immediately melts and I have to move on. A flick, a flap, a flashing transparent wing: I look for it out my truck window, any sign that will tell me winter will soon come.

Snow starts far up in the sky with one dust mote cart-wheeling through cloud. As it free-falls, moisture encarnal-izes dust: faceted crystals are born. The one becomes many and they go where wind goes: everywhere and down and touching.

I call about the cabin I was to rent near the Canadian border, but it's mired in a springlike thaw, the owner tells me. "There was snow," he says, "but it melted. The river never froze and the valley floor is open."

As I drive rain comes instead: wild midwinter tempests with thunder and lightning. Sleet punctures holes in the season. In the mountains where glaciers have retreated to tiny patches of ice, sun and wind crusts over what's left of avalanching cornices.

I stretch my legs by a lake; wind rattles the reeds where early-arriving ducks will nest. Dry, dry, the reeds sing. Six years of drought turn to seven. My own weathers are change-able: cold when I'm tired, enervated when I'm hot, ardent the farther north I drive, even without snow.

My truck rides the rise and fall of the northern Rockies. Fi-nally there's a winter blast, but wind dries it, and snow goes like a dress being torn from a corpse. When I reach Gary's cabin in northern Montana, meltwater ponds wet our legs to the shins. Snow fleas cluster in ditch water and drown. A cloud comes. It caresses the river like a feather boa, then slides across a running ridgetop. Fat flakes fall but sun shines through them like a flashlight, one transparency piercing another. No excuse for false innocence, someone says. A war is about to begin. Snow stops as if each flake had been caught by hand and thrown away with no regard for human life. The day ends. We feel bereaved before anyone dies. A curtain of sunlight falls that both hides and reveals.

In Alberta I find more of the same: open water, bare ground and at best, snow corrupted by unseasonable rain. I call friends in Alaska; they're basking in warm weather like seals. The question keeps coming up: Is this global warming or just a quirk of weather, a natural fluctuation within a larger one? Meanwhile, the east coast of North America is being blasted with strong storms.

Finally I give up my northbound journey and turn south again feeling slightly defeated. Surely, I'll find winter somewhere. The Blackfeet Indians called the Rockies "the backbone of the world." Of the Blackfeet god who brought winter, Jim Welch wrote: "Cold Maker came down from Always Winter Land. He came with the wind. He was all dressed up in white furs and he was riding a white horse. He carried a lance made of ice and a shield of hoarfrost that one could see through. . . . His laughter sounded like ice breaking up on the river."

———

Crossing into Wyoming, I climb from four thousand feet to eight thousand in elevation. On the rim of Yellowstone Park a cloud appears on the road in front of the truck. As it lifts, snow falls from it. I stop the truck, get out, and Gaby and I do a little dance of gratitude on the road. Now we're inside the cloud, and snow twists out of the sky at the windshield. Am I driving through a world that is coming apart or one that is piecing itself back together? Either way, I'm home.

At the end of the day I arrive at John and Lucy's log cabin not far from where mine is being built. They've agreed to let me live there for as long as I want. It's twelve feet by fourteen feet, with no kitchen, no bathroom, just a room big enough for a bed, a sheepherder's wood-burning cookstove, and a small desk at a south-facing window. As night comes on, the temperature hovers at zero. I split kindling, start a fire, make the bed: flannel sheets, three wool blankets, and a down sleeping bag. The window looks out on a white pasture, a buried fence, and a willow-choked stream where a moose is grazing. The north window swallows storms. I'm wildly happy. Gaby lies outside on the covered porch, surveying my friends' three dogs, four horses, plus the moose and two coyotes. Then she comes in and joins me on the bed.

Winter sets in. Cold Maker is here. He comes with wind that blows out the sun. Sun no longer erases what the season lays down. In the high country, accumulation goes on effortlessly. Right here three feet on the level pile up to four. Snowflakes are shorn of their wings and end up bald-headed, like ball bearings. Wind takes up what's left and, like dust, blows it around.

With snow a curtain of words flutters down. One day does not lead to another. Storm after storm comes, and the wind slips out from between them until the snow goes flat, compressing a whole year into one white day.

2

Seclusion, intimacy, ceremony, cabin fever—that's what winter brings. The Blackfeet made winter camps in the wide valleys below the Rockies. They wore buffalo robes with the hair on the inside and put their tents in among groves of pines or cottonwoods to protect themselves from harsh weather. They were often there for five months or "however long Cold Maker wanted to keep us," they said.

In Arnhem Land in northern Australia, the Yolngu called winter *dharratharrmirri*, meaning "having shivering." The Navajo god Hastseyalti covered travelers with *tsayelbelkladi*, a blanket of darkness that kept them warm. A Tibetan teacher promised to teach me *tumo*, how to raise my core body temperature at will. I never learned. Now I have Gaby to keep me warm.

I once spent part of a winter in Kyoto and often visited two Noh mask carvers. Mornings I watched them carve, afternoons I attended Noh theater rehearsals. The plays and their performances had a seasonality: winter was associated with north, black, tortoise, water, and mountain. We sat on tatami. There were no chairs. The stage was a ritual space, semidark, with the grassy smell of fresh tatami—like summer—wafting into my nose.

Being winter-bound means that snow's mirror reduces the simultaneity of perception to a simplicity. The wobbles and mind-jumps don't show. The sky goes black, and winter life is secret. The ground grows dizzyingly white, a wide nothingness. Darkness pulls over like a monk's cowl, enclosing us in worlds where strange things take place, where anything can happen, where the mind goes where it's never gone before, and stays.

## 3

Today the snow on the cabin roof slides, then freezes into a bowed curtain at the eaves with a fringe of icicles. Inside, rime crusts the windows. From an oval at the center, I peer out: new-fallen snow is a plain of sparks; a magpie picks lice from the moose's back, then scratches snow off the fence post and settles there. The day is short. I ride with John to the elk feed ground. He harnesses a team of black Percherons, loads the hay wagon, and feeds the elk. Fifty bulls and two hundred females come to eat. As we bump along, seven more bulls wind down a steep hill of aspens. I push flakes of hay off the back of the wagon. On the way home we put on snowshoes and hand-carry hay to a yearling that lost her way and became separated from the herd. This whole valley is under John's careful watch. He doesn't own it; he simply cares for whatever comes this way.

"Once there was so much snow here in the winters, you never saw a fence line," John says ruefully. "You could walk out the second story of your house. We fed cattle in tunnels bulldozed through snow, and lived in the dark. Now we're lucky if we get three feet on the level." He cuts a hole in the ice on a small lake and brings home trout for dinner. In winter, fish regulate their own heat, he tells me. There's tissue in their brain that keeps the head at a constant 28 degrees Celsius.

The rest of the day snow is all that happens. The moose wanders. Earlier in the week John's truck broke down. When he tried to hitchhike home, not a single car passed, so he walked the ten miles. While others leave the valley to avoid winter, John, Lucy, Rita, Jaime, Jim, Dorothy, Mark, Pat, and a handful of others stay. "It's the best time to be here," they agree.

Past midnight silence squeaks. It's been dark since four-thirty. Snow has stalled. Once in a while an errant flake tumbles down and my woodstove answers by belching smoke into the unmoving night. My face is pale; my hands are covered with soot. I'm tired of trampling circles with my own thoughts. Water in a pan on the cookstove boils down to a sputter. I write nothing. In every season the Earth is dynamic, but winter's pandemonium can be oddly quiet. I stick my head out the door: the wood pile floats, adrift in glitter. Icicles ripple and fall from the roof. They lie on new snow like glistening sticks. The branch from which they fell . . . *where is it?* If I kept walking through the pines above this cabin, would I find a translucent tree?

Morning. Sun presses down and the ground-dazzle shivers. Right now the circumpolar migrants are getting close to the equator. The long-tailed jaeger has stopped his pirating and predation on other birds to fly. The one-and-a-half-ounce sanderling flies alongside the white-rumped sandpiper and the ruddy turnstone. Higher up, as high as twenty thousand feet, the arctic terns lead the way from winter to fish-glutted southern seas and all-night summer light.

Around here, glitter crackles, snowflakes knot and dissolve. Then a weather system's low pressure drags its feet over the valley, and wind throws snow spiraling in three-dimensional curves down the sky's cylindrical surface. Just before snow hits the roof, it falls straight and on the valley floor a new white carpet unrolls on top of the old. I get into bed with Gaby and read the legend of a man in Japan who fell through a crevasse into a bear den and was saved by the bear. Pyramids of snow sift in under the door. The geometry of winter sums up its angles at my feet.

Yet spring keeps trying to come. Wind rips clouds apart and sun makes icicles shed tears. Worldwide, spring events are now occurring two days earlier per decade, and temperature jumps accelerate the disruption of the connectedness among species. From plant to bug, to bird, to tree, to water, to fish, to bear—

it doesn't take many steps until the whole world of living things collapses. We've already lost chestnut trees, the Grand Banks fishery, elms, Monterey sardines, as well as thousands of feet of topsoil. Plants close their stomata in reaction to hotter than usual days; if closed to long, the plants will overheat and die. Since greenhouse gases remain in the air for one hundred years, whatever we do now to stop the planet from getting warmer will not be felt right away. Meanwhile, the land is getting hotter and drier, the seas are growing, the ice caps in Greenland and Antarctica that hold three quarters of the earth's fresh water are melting, and plants, animals, and humans are becoming more disease-ridden. Increased rainfall is expected to wash more soil and crops away; prolonged drought will scorch already arid lands. Besides water shortages, there will be shortages of food. In the newspaper I read of Band-Aid stopgaps to the rising oceans: enormous gates that will be closed across the entrances to seaports in the Netherlands and in Venice.

Here, I look out the cabin window: a north wind splinters the broken bones of fallen snowflakes to ice. I strap on snowshoes, climb the hill behind the cabin, and push my head into flocked pine trees. The verb *to pine* comes from a different root than the noun, *pinus,* for the tree (though, with *root,* we're still using botanical language here). *Pinus* comes from the Latin verb *poena,* meaning "superseded by pain."

Winter is about evanescence: absences stack up, and the starkness of living alone with almost no family as background noise is, itself, falling snow that has escaped being pressed into the glacier's time machine. Looking out the door, I see nothing and no one except the black-and-white magpie that flaps from one end of the sky to the other as if bringing winter back every time it tries to disappear.

4

I first came to Wyoming in the winter of 1975. By January 1976 I was filming in a lambing shed on a 250,000-acre sheep-and-cattle ranch. The first day I was there a solar eclipse darkened the sun and the sheep bedded down the way they do at nightfall. Twenty below dropped to 30 below. When the sun returned, roosters crowed and the sheep stood, yawned, and began their day all over again.

Starting over again was what I would soon be doing. The man I was to marry died of cancer that October. Afterward, I stayed on and bought a ranch. Sixteen winters came and went. Extreme cold was most terrifying and most beguiling. The sound of cattle and horses eating all night long to stay warm kept me awake, as well as the white-eyed blizzards, the shake-down of adamantine frost fall.

Winter on a cattle ranch means there are newborn calves warming up in the kitchen, round-the-clock watches for first-calf heifers, and middle-of-the-night rescues of neighbors stuck in a snowdrift. One night we had to rescue a newborn calf from the jaws of a hungry coyote. Its legs were on the other side of the fence and had been gnawed on. I shooed the coyote away, and we carried the calf to the barn, where she was doctored, warmed up, and fed with a bottle.

Another night one of my dogs, Rusty (the father of Sam), led me to a herd of elk that had bedded down in the upper pasture, just for the joy of showing them to me. We managed the ranch not for high productivity but for the health of the ground. We ranched sunlight and grass. The elk, birds, deer, humans, cattle, horses, cougars, bears, coyotes, and dogs that lived there benefited.

The ranch house was a hundred-year-old, uninsulated monstrosity that I hated. The plumbing and electricity had been jerry-rigged into place, and in winter it was hard to keep water flowing. To take a bath, I had to heat the tub with a space heater to keep the first bit of water that flowed from the tap from freezing to the bottom.

Mild frostbite was common. I wore arctic boots at the dinner table. One day I rescued a bull that had fallen through the ice on the lake. Night was coming on, it was 20 below, and he was soaking wet, so I pushed him into the cattle squeeze and dried him off using a pink hair dryer connected by a couple of hundred yards of extension cord plugged in at the house.

Sometimes, in the winter, other people's sheep and cows came off the mountain into our back pasture, and we'd feed them until the owners could trail them home in the spring. Our ranch was at the base of a cirque in the mountains, and our pastures were the natural catch pens for strays.

Winter is not just bone-aching cold and white skies. It's the complexities of the season that I love. Sometimes at the ranch warm winds blasted through in January. Steam rose up the rock faces of mountains, while veils of gray clouds wafted by. A black cloud hung over the waterfall. Icicles dripped, then re-froze into wild, bent-back daggers. I had four hours of chores in the morning, two at night. In between, I wrote.

There were almost no visitors and few forays to town. Winter confinement could be excruciating. If winter means going inward, it also involves the barbs and stings of the place to which you are confined. But the demands of the season and animals returned me to sanity. A bum calf would need feeding, or a wild heifer would have to be brought to the calving barn. The only way to get her in was to think like her, to anticipate her terror. Inside the barn, I played Chopin nocturnes to calm myself, as well as the cows. My own itches left me then, and I could give myself over wholly to the needs of the animals. Later, the northern lights would pulse up—we had a pledge among friends to wake each other if the aurora showed. I knew then that what I had, where I lived, was enough.

But things change. Now I live in another part of the state on the skeletal remains of a glacier. Hundreds of scoured-out kettle ponds surround me. Some have water, some do not. Sand-hill cranes, trumpeter swans, and Canada geese summer in the ones that do. It is a place famous for its snowy winters.

My neighbor John says, "The winter of 1986 was the biggest snow year I can remember. Hell, when we shoveled the snow off the roof, we had to fling it upward! It snowed eighteen inches every night, and by the end of the first three weeks of winter, there was nine feet on the ground. To go anywhere was to go down a tunnel. We'd plow a lane to feed the cows and then it'd snow all night and more snow would blow in and bury them. Once the snow slid off the roof and buried ten or twelve yearlings. Another time the cows were crossing the river and the ice broke. They fell in and were trapped in the water. In thirteen minutes, all thirty-five head died, right in front of me. At the house we had to shovel out holes where the windows were, and one for the chimney. A lane had to be plowed from the front door to the barn and the garage, and from there, all the way to the highway—about five miles."

Up until the 1950s, mail was delivered by dogsled, pulled not by huskies but by Airedales. "It's what we had in our back-yard, and so they got used," Dorothy, a ninety-six-year-old resident, tells me. She and her husband did all the mail deliveries here. He's gone now, and she lives on her own, splits wood, guts trout, and bakes bread.

By chance, a young couple I once neighbored with twenty-two years ago are now neighbors again. I met Mark and Pat Domek at the beginning of the third-worst winter in the history of Wyoming: 1978–79. We'd rented run-down, side-by-side, one-room cabins on an abandoned ranch. The snow came on November 7 and didn't disappear until late April. It heaped up around our cabins like wings, and the nighttime temperatures dropped to 60 degrees below zero. Mark and Pat were newlyweds then. Sometimes I'd tie a note to Rusty's collar and send him to their cabin. It read: "Can I come for dinner?" Or, "Please come over here."

The cold made the winter seem lonelier. My fiancé had died of cancer, and I was broke. No parka, no Sorel Paks, one pair of cheap long underwear. Cold was the crucible from which I had to rise. It stood for the brokenness of my life—the loss of the man I loved. I had no neat stack of firewood, no meat to eat. Extreme cold and a feeling of bewilderment became forever linked. If I could survive the winter, I could survive David's death.

Some weeks I helped ranchers feed cattle. The snow was so deep there were no fence posts in sight. To get to the stack yards took all morning; feeding hay in lanes plowed by a D9 bulldozer took the rest of the day. We'd get frostbite on our hands, cheeks, noses, ears, and toes. After feeding, we'd cuddle on a couch by the woodstove—not for sexual pleasure but simply to warm each other after a whole day outside.

The rest of the winter I stayed in, with one mandatory walk a day along the frozen North Fork of the Shoshone River. The rest of the time I read and reread most of Faulkner, García Márquez, Kawabata Yasunari, Steinbeck, Camus, Octavio Paz, Thoreau, and Emerson, plus all the medieval Chinese and Japanese poetry in translation I could get my hands on. I thought of them as winter poems—not about winter, necessarily, but written in a dark time. In *Poems of the Late T'ang*, I learned that Shih Huang-ti, an emperor in 221 B.C., tried to build a bridge over the sea to see where the sun rose. In the poems of Li Ho, blue raccoons wept blood, the God of Rain rode into autumn pools, green flames rose from an owl's nest. Describing the coming of winter, he wrote: "In the slime of desolate moors the floods of autumn whitened."

I pored over books of Sung and T'ang dynasty paintings. The painters and writers of the time were often victims of political turmoil, and their inked images of remote valleys and deep forests stood for the way the natural world soaked up their anguish, disillusionment, bewilderment, sudden losses, and consequent solitude. Their paintings were emblematic. In those spindly mountains and etched valleys, lines of trees and bamboo forests, and tiny human-made pavilions there was a hallucinatory balance, a clear track out of reckless exhilaration and despair. I too had withdrawn from the world and turned my energies toward ink on paper—both painting and writing. Semisuicidal and unable to sleep at night, I'd peer at those landscapes by flashlight. Though stylized, they emitted a fresh sense; they were places to which I could go in my mind's eye. They never failed to save me.

That was two decades ago. Now Pat is the town's postmaster and Mark is building a cabin for me. I still beg dinners from them on lonely evenings, and when Sam was still alive he liked to lie at Mark's feet as if out of some genetic memory passed from canine father to son. Despite the long interlude, we still fit into each other's lives with ease. The hard winter of

1978–79 has turned into something sweet, a raison d'être, not a reason for suicide.

## 5

I'm wrong when I say "nothing is happening." For the time being my movements are being restricted by a pissed-off moose outside my window. There's snow up to her hocks. Her back is bleached brown; she has patches of darker hair on her ribs, a pale underbelly, and a loose, hanging lip. The too-long ears and slender legs are specially insulated with internal oils to keep them warm. She has no calf and nibbles on red twigs with tight buds. Perhaps she's hungry; a winter diet of willows isn't very nourishing.

John, a sturdy, no-nonsense outdoorsman of Norwegian descent, admits that the moose had him cornered last week, and Lucy had to drive fifty yards from the house to the barn so he could jump into her car. "It's the easiest rescue I've ever made," Lucy says. She's what John calls "an ambulance jockey," an EMT who regularly saves lives.

The moose eyes us, then drops her head and goes on eating. "The moose is what you have to watch out for," John says. "They can be more dangerous than bears or wolves. They don't scare off, and if they're mad, stay out of their way."

I lie alone in the cabin. Wedged between the humps of a moraine, I imagine a mountain of ice grinding by, dredging thousands of feet of dirt and rock and dropping house-sized boulders in its wake as it backs away.

Nothing of the kind is happening. On the contrary, snow stacks up and two ravens feast on a road-killed elk. Cold-adapted animals are snuggling in their subnivian empires. Snow is a wonderful insulator. It provides emergency shelter for ruffed grouse and ptarmigan. Grizzlies are in their dens having babies. Like bears who delay the implantation of the embryo until winter, martens, minks, long-tailed weasels, ermines, wolverines, spotted skunks, badgers, and river otters do the same.

Light struggles to return. Since December 21, the days began to widen, hope resumed, no matter how low the temperatures were and how bad the evening news. My sheepherder friends always said, "Let's just hope we make it to green grass again."

## 6

Snow emits light. We just can't see the long wavelength of heat energy, but it's there. Snow is a "black body" that absorbs 100 percent of the energy incident upon it. As trees and bushes sponge in heat, molecules begin jumping. The temperature of the tree trunks, branches, and leaves rises. The warmth makes snow melt and slump and the hollows around boulders and at the bottom of trees widen.

A foot of snow falls in the night and shifts uncomfortably under its own weight. The open collar around sage and willow fills in. Errant snowflakes dart around the yard as if lost. Gaby tries to catch one and finally succeeds. It dissolves in

her mouth, and she cocks her head in wonderment. Just up
the hill, snow-laden pines drop their loads into deep drifts,
and Gaby wonders how such explosions of white could be so
silent.

In the morning I deliver a bag of fish to our neighbor
Dorothy. In the afternoon I snowshoe to the river. A channel
in a nearby stream opens briefly. Riffles break around a beaver
dam and trap bubbles under ice. In midstream bunched crystals
twirl and chime: candle ice. I jump onto a gravel island whose
snow has gone sugary. On both sides, water pours out from
under green lids. Ice ticks, splits, rings like a distant phone, and
refreezes. Once, flying over Ellesmere Island, I saw down
through a vertical stack of blue ice that had frozen and re-
frozen at the foot of a mountain like a storehouse of separate
rivers, each one waiting to flow again.

Downstream I search for ducks. There are none. The trunks
of old willows are striated—white with gray—arboreal hy-
phens between what words? *Water. Shade. Desire. Mallard.* Up
by the highway, the huge osprey nest on top of a telephone
pole holds only snow.

The layers of white settle as days go by. Wind and occasional
sun do their work on drifts. When the snow crusts over, I un-
buckle my snowshoes, step into skis, and make the six-mile
round trip to my unfinished cabin. Then I see coyote tracks
and follow them. I love coyotes because, unlike the hierarchy-
obsessed wolf, they hang loose. Bachelors have their own society but help out harried mothers when the pups are born. Once

a New York editor asked me to investigate why coyotes howl. After following them around for a winter and talking to biologists who had studied them for years, I couldn't really give a reason why. When not vocalizing to declare their geographical position or calling to a mate, they seemed to howl just for the hell of it. Why not? As if insulted by the coyote's sense of fun, the editor killed the story.

Overhead, clouds boil. The deeper into the snowy mountains I go, the happier I am. The Japanese word *oku* means not only "north" but also "deep," "inner," "the heart of a mountain," "to penetrate to the depth of something or someone," "the bottom of one's heart," and "the end of one's mind."

When the sun comes out, Gaby and I use my snowshoes as seats and bask in the sun like two seals. Our planet rotates around a sun that is rotting, the rotation itself in the midst of its 100,000-year change. The ellipsis of the orbit is taking us through the spiral arm of the Orion nebula. At any moment we could be pelted by asteroids—a sudden blackness approaching, then *wham:* all megafauna would become extinct.

We don't need any extra excitement; we've created our own. We are living in the midst of a holocaust of extinctions that goes unmentioned because the victims are not held captive in one spot and can't use language.

Moving again, Gaby and I pass through a stand of old aspens that are wind-tortured and wavy, as if they've been trembling for a hundred years. Below are the beginnings of my log cabin. It's a one-man project: Mark cut the standing dead trees, milled them, debarked them, shaped each to fit one on top of the other. From a rocky knob, I watch the walls rising slowly. He says, "This is how we take a dead tree and make it grow again."

7

A week later. The moose has gone and has been replaced by a bear. John points to the hill behind my cabin. "Go see for yourself." Under a white knob a yearling black bear is curled up in the snow taking a nap. Bears are partial hibernators. They wake often, go outside their dens, ramble around, go back in again. Wakefulness comes not simply from warmer weather but as a result of the way their cold-adapted bodies work. In the winter the bear brain gets glucose from ketones made from the fat in the liver instead of from proteins. But livers are toxic-waste dumps: as soon as the toxicity gets too high, an internal alarm rouses the bear. He wakes up, leaves his den, and goes hunting for a proper meal.

When I snowshoe by, the bear opens his eyes, wipes the side of his face with his paw, looks at me, sniffs the air, then goes back to sleep. He's a small bear, not yet fully grown. His black coat is sleek and snow-dusted. A curved bank in the snow-drift fits him like a pillow. He makes snow look like a warm place to snooze. One paw goes over the top of his head, rubbing his small ear. There's a deep in-breath, then a low, snuffling sigh. I crouch down. Oh, how I'd like to lie down next to him, to be (as in the arctic legend) the woman who married the bear.

Clouds float, the temperature warms, and four feet of snow on the ground settles to three. It's become fashionable to seek out or retell the worst extremes of weather and travel, as if simply living—wherever we are—isn't juicy enough. I've endured much colder winters than this one. I was in Fairbanks, Alaska, in January 1989 when a Siberian blast dropped the temperature from minus 52 degrees Fahrenheit to minus 82 degrees along the Tanana River. There were only a few hours of daylight. My breath froze; the town of Fairbanks was encased in a hard fog that crackled like fire. Tires went square, a friend's retina popped out, contact lenses couldn't be worn, a child's tongue became frozen to the school-bus window and had to be cut away from the glass with a scalpel.

Our faces had to be covered at all times. I learned not to cough or laugh outside. My skis wouldn't work—not enough lubricity in the snow. Such temperatures reminded me that extreme cold is just like the great heat of a desert. Some sort of moisture—and therefore, warmth—is necessary to make things work, to enable skis to slide, to create an environment where living and breathing is possible.

Ten days later, when it warmed up to minus 20 degrees, the air felt almost tropical. We skied up to a hot spring and helped bathe a baby born to a hippie couple two nights earlier when it was 75 degrees below zero. Even so, getting into the hot water was excruciating. Our bodies had become cold-hardened, and sudden heat was almost more than we could bear.

The Alaskan cold followed me back to Wyoming that year.

The water pipes at the ranch froze, and the nail heads inside the house were capped with frost. Calving had just begun. It was only minus 45 degrees Fahrenheit, but calves were freezing to the ground as soon as they were born. I had to attend each birth to make sure the mother cows got their calves up in time, which meant almost no sleep for me at all.

By comparison, it feels cozy here with John and Lucy next-door, and our dogs, horses, the elk, moose, and bear, all part of our winter society. This is "a global warming winter," John says. "Not as much snow as we used to have, but enough for us to remember the ways cold and snow rule our days."

In the morning John sets out on skis for one of the lakes near his house. He cuts a hole in the ice and catches enough trout for dinner. "He knows winter the way other people know the layout of a town," Lucy tells me. "He knows where the elk are, which ones didn't make it to the feed ground, how many wolves there are, and of course, where the fish will be. Like, which side of which pond they'll be on, and the day he can begin finding them there."

Over a trout dinner we tell stories of days and nights living in wall tents with snow leaning in on all sides, Coleman lamps hissing, foot-wide warm streams gurgling by; of trying to keep the collapsible woodstove from collapsing, and waiting hours for food to cook over what John calls "squaw fires" at ten thousand feet. But it's the do-nothing hours of tent life that we miss the most, hours when we simply listened. Up through the river wind and tree hush and the sneezing, squall-ing storms came the whistling grunts of bugling elk, so eerie and sexual. We watched snow stack up and talked to animals, making their calls our own.

## 8

Two ravens make black *X*'s in the sky; a horse is snoring. My head is filled with the pots-and-pans clapping-and-bolting gurgle of internal gossip, not about people but about the dogs and horses I've worked with and known. My current bout of what sheepherders used to call "people-phobia" should worry me, but it doesn't. I like a strong binge of socializing, followed by a few months of monastic quiet—as long as I can be with animals. My older sister reminds me of the nights she'd come home from parties to find the family dog neatly tucked under the covers, head on the pillow, while I slept on the floor.

Solitude becomes a reflex. Instead of calling friends when I'm lonely, I shy away from them. On the other hand, solitude is highly overrated. We've romanticized Thoreau's days on Walden Pond, forgetting that he ate with the Emersons most evenings. The famous "examined life" included dinners and intelligent conversation with extraordinary neighbors, and I admit, I long for that now. People who have lived where the winter weather is truly harsh—like the Arctic—know that solitude is anathema to mental health and is inevitably linked to suicide. I concur. But living with animals is something else again.

On the ranch where I lived, I'd lie in the snowfields with the cows at midday, leaning my head against their bulging, pregnant bodies. I'd search out coyote dens, sit above the entrance, and wait for the pups to wander out. There were colts and working dogs being born and growing up, and cougars and bears on the benchlands above the pastures. Then and now, I apprentice myself to birds and animals, spending days trying to learn the way they know about one another and about my state of mind. My dog Rusty knew when something was wrong during calving. One night he pawed at my arm during dinner until I followed him outside to a distant pasture where a cougar was crouched by the cows and young calves. The mother cows had formed a wall and were pacing back and forth between their calves and the cougar. I made a lot of noise and scared the cougar away. Other days, the "using horses," as they are called, always seem to know what's up. "Hell, that horse knows you're coming out to the corral to catch him before you even get out of bed," Ray Hunt, the horse trainer, said. But how?

Life with animals sponges up our human arrogance. We're not the only ones who "know," and we're anything but alone. There's a great sensory mechanism at work in the world: millions of noses, eyes, and ears, and nonhuman howls, bugles, grunts, screams, and song.

I'm still grieving about a recent loss, and winter helps me with the job. My journal from September reads: "Facing the darkness, a hummingbird comes to visit because my dog has died."

Before the writing of this book was begun, Sam began faltering. We were making our daily hike following two string lakes in the mountains. He kicked up dust with wobbly legs. At the willow-choked stream that feeds the lake, he lay on green moss among wildflowers, one leg resting on glacial till, the other dipped into floury water. In those hours everything ticked—springs dripped, wind stirred dew inside the cups of harebells. Noctilucent clouds shone in the north. We walked home as the sun was setting.

Later, in the night, I lay on my sleeping bag and watched Sam breathing, knowing we wouldn't have too much more time together. I pondered all that he had tried to teach me: wild enthusiasm, rustic joy, easygoing love, and unconditional living.

We were living in our tent. Below, a well was being dug for my cabin, and Sammy, Gaby, and I went down to watch the activity. In one hour the derrick went up and the drill augured down. Jim, the driller, said, "We have to use a diamond bit to go through these erratics. The glaciers put a lot of rock down here, but they also left a lot of water."

The drilling of the well was like running through pages in nature's book, each deposition, each shelf of rock, a turning page. Under the rolling shell-bed was a layer of loose-grained sand and gravel, then tight gravel, then more shells, then a gigantic "page" of granite.

Jim hit water at 150 feet, where it lay in horizontal bands between depositions, but he went deeper. What he was doing was bringing up the collapsed history of ice ages, and the warm, shallow seas that came before and after. The diamond bit went deep. Down there, Jim told me, are mountains and rivers, oceans and beaches, glaciers and fires. The water, when it came, was blue-gray and looked like flannel. It turned muddy, then gray-green. The flow lessened, then surged, and the water came clean. Sam, Gaby, and I lay on the excavated sand and drank from the pipe.

Our tent faced the mountains, its screened window a perfect triangle. Through it the moon was a half-eaten orange. My attention was fully focused on Sam; we were idle and together all day long. As a result, the world slowed as if Earth had paused in her massive rotation. Every tiny thing loomed large: flies coming to life in a sunny window and the ones on their backs, their legs wheeling as they died. The days were real, Sam was real, and his death would be real too.

It was August, and on a Friday a brutal wind blew all afternoon. I had offered to take a friend's mother to a luncheon on a remote ranch. When I returned, friends from California—Robin, Jim, and their son, Crister, were at my camp. But something was terribly wrong. They were crouching over Sam. He was having a grand mal seizure. He had lesions in his brain from being hit by lightning with me years earlier. Since then he had become prone to mild seizures. But this one had him thrashing, and it would not stop. By the time I found a vet, two hours had gone by.

He lay in a cage at the local clinic for six days. The seventh day, Gary came down from Montana to be with me. When we arrived at the clinic the next morning, I was shocked to see Sam sitting up. When I called out his name, he turned and looked at me. He'd been lying flat for six days; he'd been deaf for six months. Now, suddenly, unbelievably, he could move and hear.

At noon Gary and I put Sam in the clinic's outside pen to lie in the sun, then went to lunch. When we came back, Sam was walking around and sniffing. He heard us coming, turned and looked at us as if to say, get me the hell out of here. I called Brent, the vet, to come outside. He said he'd never seen a recovery like this before. He hugged me, he hugged Sam. The emergency passed; Gary returned to Montana.

Sam and I went home that night. He slept soundly on his bed next to mine. Part of the reason I'd opted to live in a tent was so we could be together at dog level, and the arrangement had pleased him. Three days passed. Sam wobbled and walked, lapped up the buffalo broth I made for him, sniffed flowers, and slept. I had to go away for a night and left Sam in the care of friends with whom he had often stayed. The next morning he crashed. I felt overwhelmed by guilt. I raced to the clinic where he'd been taken. For ten hours I sat with him. By evening he was dead.

My neighbors Rita and Jamie came for me. Rita drove my pickup, and I held Sam on my lap. I talked to him, draped over my knees, all the way home. Mark was at the cabin. When he saw Sam, he quietly grabbed a shovel. I hadn't thought where to bury him, but the moment we drove in, I knew. Across a swale from the cabin's south-facing window seat, there's an eight-foot-high boulder erratic, deposited there during the last ice age. The rock stands alone on a knob below a cirque of eleven-thousand-foot mountains. It's lion colored and dappled with lichen. A crease runs down the middle like Sam's furrowed brow.

Mark, Rita, Jaime, and I took turns digging Sam's grave. I held him for a long time, then wrapped him in his red blanket. He was still warm when I laid him in the earth. A small white rock, dug up from the well, marks his grave.

9

That was six months ago. Now it's late winter and there's a full moon. From John and Lucy's cabin I drive to the end of the drifted-in lane and ski to Sam's grave. The moon is so bright it looks like the sun. Snow is deep, soft in some places and in others hard drifts. The crust breaks open; I plunge in. Changing from skis to snowshoes, I still sink deep. Yet a path opens up, no matter which way my webbed feet turn. The way is lumpy, mountainous, bare, an undulating circuit into white. Over the lip of a moraine, I come to my unfinished cabin and, across the way, the boulder where Sam is buried.

The moon is an eye watching us. Gaby and I start for the grave. But the snow is deep and I sink down. Fumbling for incense and matches, I realize my fingers are wet. The incense breaks and the matches fail to light. While walking among the dead one is supposed to envision drinking amrita from skull cups, but right now I only want to summon Sam's ghost and make sure the red blanket in which he's buried is still keeping him warm. I want to hold him again.

A few more steps and I'm up to my waist in snow, then down in it. Am I sinking into a storm? I flail ridiculously, then catch myself. Gaby is thrashing too. She stands on my feet like a child learning to dance. When I fall again, something breaks inside me.

Back across the swale we go to the unfinished cabin. Inside, I light a Coleman stove and melt snow in a pan for water. How many hundreds of times have I done this? In Greenland villages, ice is hacked from stranded icebergs and left stacked behind each house like cordwood to be melted for drinking water.

Gaby drinks snow water and I sip tea. We are hiding from the power of dark energy that's threatening to rip apart the cosmos; we teeter on the edge of time at the event horizon of a black hole embedded in a hot cauldron of gases equal to 2.6 million suns. We are told of a dark, circular shadow where the rays pass through, never again to emerge. We worship a sun that is killing itself and will be gone in 5 million years, first collapsing, then expanding uncontrollably until the seas boil away and Earth becomes a charred ember.

I tell these things to Gaby, but she doesn't care. Satiated, she lies on her back, paws up, and smiles. I turn off the stove and stretch out on the cold floor beside her. Outside, a few flakes drift down and a wind picks up. Slowly, slowly, snow fills in our tracks, erasing the dog-and-human lineage of Sam senior to Rusty senior to Rusty junior to Sam, and the circle of Mark, Pat, and me.

———

A burr pricks me. I pluck it from under my leg and hold it up: its stickers are arranged in spirals. Rotate it one way, it's a universe auguring inward. Rotate it the other way, it's the riptide of dark energy tearing the burr apart. I toss it and step into my skis. Every second is a universe. Gaby barks. Snow glistens as far as the eye can see.

I dawdle the rest of the day, skiing around, napping on snowbanks, whittling a stick that a beaver has already whittled. To touch winter this way—with my elbows and back and hair—is to operate on desolation, sew it up with tropical sinew, and solder it with sun-fires.

Late in the day the sun glazes mountains, valleys, rivers, and ponds with a pearl-powder shine. Sagebrush pops up as if it had grown suddenly. Earth breathes, leaving behind a faint scent. The place where Sam is buried is a view of the world without end. It is the center and the edge of time; it's the place where eyelids fall away. I'd like to be buried beside him.

Finally Gaby and I head for the highway. The sun's last gasp is a flare of pink that torches a path upward to a dissolving cloud. By the time I reach the road, the stripe has loosened into a ruffle. Dusk comes and the pink slips from sight—just like the way Sam left the world. Night is a regular uncertainty.

10

It's March. Dawn light is the color of snow. Snow looks like day. Day is bent sideways by red willows that are ribbed with white. South-facing eaves drip; north-facing eaves are hung with icicles. It snows everywhere. In the cab of my pickup, I listen to the news. The war with Iraq is imminent. We're so good at making war on each other, but peace is difficult. We humans are addicted to conflict; we make war on lovers, friends, neighbors, and nations of plants, animals, bugs, fish, and human tribes. We want things our way and now. It's hard to understand that all such tensions are really the dynamic expression of union.

Out the window, a magpie alights on a moose's back. Under the snow, extended families of muskrats huddle together to stay warm; I make dinner for John while Lucy is on call; five snow crystals combine to make a single snowflake that falls; ravens nest communally. Winter teaches us cooperative living, not war.

Later. I ski down to the frozen river. A cloud lies over it like a feather boa—soft over hard, mist over river ice. I ponder the Diné (Navajo) words that can mean two opposing things at once: the word for "up" can also mean "down." Everywhere in nature I see opposites moving toward resolution. Species do not compete but rather cooperate within a natural hierarchy.

A wind comes from the north and blows out the sun. Winter begins again. I split more wood and light a cooking fire. A curtain falls: it is a snowbank sliding. I think of the economic and political lessons of the glaciers I saw at the other end of the world. Here, planes of light shift mountain shadows up one cliff, then erase them from the opposite wall. I rattle back across the icy ski track. The sky darkens and the moon rises. Unlike the sun, the moon worships us, while we "civilized" beings make "progress" by perpetuating rolling waves of destruction against every living thing—the entire sentient world—and, in so doing, kill what tenderness resides in us.

A hundred years ago a Zuni predicted that at the end of the world there would be famine. "It is already in our midst but we can't see it because it's hidden by the false bounty of the stores. At the end, our tools and technologies will rise against us. The stars will fall and we will all be boiled by hot rain."

After snow, clouds slide up the valley like smoke, and salt sage holds tiny lights of frost, lording over bunchgrass. The blue wisps of alpine fescue look like smoke: what will be left of the world after being ravaged by fires. A raven grooms herself on a glacial erratic cocked sideways. Long ago, glaciers seeded this valley with boulders and stones, broadcasting them like pieces of time—old biscuits and discarded ideas. "You stay here, while I go on," the glacier said, dropping an armload of granite, tipping its hip and shoulder, lowering its head until all the rock had slipped from her.

The same is true in human love: one stays, one goes; there are successes and failures. It does not matter which way the glacier stepped or if she maintained her equilibrium. There are always these deposits being made. Gift or insult to stability?

Which are they? Perhaps both. As in any movement—a walk, a waltz, or a leap of love—the grace is in how boldly we falter. The awkwardness itself is the dance: a stepping forward, a slipping back, a storm pitching over the notched cirque of a mountain wall until sun reappears.

*Part Three*

# THE UNFASTENED:
# ON THE SPANISH RIVER

John and Lucy invite me on a "winter float." They like to be the first ones on the river. It's 12 degrees and the river is covered by ice. We drag the canoe through deep snow, and wait. An eagle flies a perfect circle above us as the day warms. People on the other side of the globe are killing each other, but here, the earth is just waking up: a stunted icefall starts to thaw, a bruised avalanche chute sheds white curds and wisps, an island in the stream bursts through its miniature ice cap.

There's a thrumming *whonk*: the river ice shifts. "Let's go," John whispers. We slide the canoe off the snowbank and bang it onto a crack until water leaks through. Panes of ice wheel from the bow, like the workings of a clock churning suddenly. My mind's sheer cliffs lie flat. World-sorrow drowns. River water runs, the color of fish skin and kiwi sorbet. Riffles chatter, clouds part. When the sun comes, the river takes it as its own, and the canoe floats on top of that burning.

Ahead we hear shallow water running fast. John steers left, aiming for deeper water, and we glide a blue, sluicing channel that puts us on a collision course with a rock. I'm in the front of the boat, digging in hard with my paddle, but John's geometry isn't working. We hit the midstream boulder, tip, and fall.

A duck flies up. There's green by my ear. Water floods in. I'm on my back in frigid water that finds its way to my skin. John stands. He's laughing. His camera case is floating downstream. Lucy extricates herself from under the canoe's middle strut, spitting water. "Were you just going to let me drown?" she asks. John smiles. We're dressed for winter, not canoeing, and our knee-high arctic boots are brimming with water.

We right the canoe and climb through thigh-deep snow among willows. The sun emerges and there's frost fall in the air: the "glitterati" have come to bring us winter cheer. The house up ahead has smoke curling from its chimney. Western hospitality dictates: we barge in, dripping, and warm up by a stranger's fire.

"How'd you like your river trip?" John asks, grinning, on the way home. We were on the water barely ten minutes. It takes the rest of the day to get warm.

2

The wind is wrong, and days go by before we can go out on the river again. In the night I wake with a strange longing: to feel cold water close over my face, for full immersion. I can't help but think about all the kinds of war we wage, and at the same time remember the river: the fractured ice, the glinting green, the startled duck, the way water let the slim hull of the canoe split open the river, and the way it flowed back together again, healed. With the melting of the ice packs, deforestation, desertification, and low snowpack, our water world is drying up. What kind of perversity allows us to create landscape as an aspect of mind and with that same mind become its destroyer? Why is there beauty?

In the morning the pissed-off moose that lives by the cabin munches willow contentedly, and the black bear on the hill takes another wintertime nap. I try to keep these rustic joys and our destruction of the natural world in mind simultaneously, but it is a tortuous practice, one that leaves me despairing.

I drive up the road to the end of the pavement, strap on snowshoes, and walk, recalling that when Anton Chekhov set out in the month of April 1890 for the island of Sakhalin, he was coughing up blood. It was a four-thousand-mile journey that lasted three months. He had only two coats, a pair of leather boots, a bottle of cognac, and a knife for "killing tigers." He wrote to his sister: "I have my fur coat on. My body is all right but my feet are freezing. I wrap them in the leather overcoat, but it is no use. I have two pair of breeches on."

I wear Polartec and step lightly in a world that is warming, even though the day is cold. Later, I tend my householder's fire and make tea, heavily smoked Lapsang souchong. How lucky I am to be able to live anywhere in the world. Yet I can be just as stuck as those without such freedoms.

Odysseus, on his way home from war, was taken by a flood, heaved onto shore, and made love to by a goddess. He survived "winter's hoary blasts," wrung out "the scum of the wild ocean" from his hair, and remained "wonder-fixed." That's my prescription for each of us. To be driven into action by the wild beauty and difficulty of a place; to make decisions about it based on biological health—what we can do for the earth— not how much money we can pimp from it.


*3*


We are following wolf tracks. The sun is out and water is leak- ing from under snowbanks at the edge of the river. The wolves traveled at dawn. There were two of them, John says. A gray wolf and one that is blackish brown. We can see where the snow inside their splayed tracks has been melted by sun and re- frozen so that now the tracks shine like dropped coins. Later, the rising moon will slide across them, followed by the shadow of the mountain, and snow will refill them until all signs of the wolves are erased. We follow the wolves into an aspen grove pinned to a slope, then lose them completely.

A crust has hardened the meadow, and we portage the green canoe across it. We're attempting to float the river again. On the bank we find more tracks. The wolves came for water. I see where they pawed at the edge, broke through ice, and licked the shards.


At water's edge, trapped bubbles wiggle. Shelves of ice that float from the sides of boulders like wings have turned to a sugary slush. We slide the canoe in and startle four swans.

They flap hard, turn midair, and disappear upstream. We let the current take us down. The river is shallow, and sun on shallow water is warped time. Past becomes present. There is no future. A six-foot-high snowbank undulates as we pass, paddling in slow time.

Panes of ice float alongside the canoe as if broken out of something we can't see. The war escalates. A war against Iraq that is self-serving and unfair. Almost two hundred years ago an Inuit man who was told about World War I asked why people who did not even know each other would fight.

Nights, I'd been reading the Norse myth Ragnarok. It begins: "An axe-age, a sword-age, shields will be gashed; there will be a wind-age and a wolf-age before the world is wrecked." By floating this river I am trying to understand the global war against the planet, against those who try to live in accord with it. I listen and look to see what, from the river, I can learn.


Winter is a time when we see into things. One minute, life is so much mush; in the next, it comes clear. We break through ice to come on more ice, one translucent door opening onto another. The construct of a single snowflake belies winter's genius: how seeming opacities translate into see-through, cartwheeling membranes that stack up and compress into ice mountains; diamond-hard sparks that slice away self-deception. If blizzards bring on oblivion, their winds also whisk it away. What's left is a swept-out room of stark beauty and clear light.

———

Mallards fly up as we move downstream. Panes of ice hit the hull of the boat, spin away, bump into others, and drive them sideways, slowing until the broken pieces of mirror merge and float as one. Each is a lesson in geometry. How many shapes can there can be?

Diamonds, swords, and goblets. That's what winter's GNP is. But the diamonds dissolve as we pass, the swords buckle, and the goblets break, joyously spilling their contents: water going back to water. Winter's starting point and font is water. Ice is water's best student; later, water learns from ice. We glide on the current of the vertical as if running across the edge of a sword. One cut and all delusion drops away.

The canoe slides through a white tunnel on a river that ticks and spits. The banks are walls of snow, sinuous depositions that sag and glisten where the sun's torch has drawn a bead on ice letting water into the seam. The river is fast, its bottom gold. We paddle until the surface smoothes out, then let the current take us. The swans and Canada geese we spooked earlier keep landing on the river just ahead. Now, each time we round a bend, we startle them again. They fly forward as if their job is to pull the river into existence for our boat.

Now we are the ice's only companions. At one shallow place the pieces surge and heave onto a glittering blockade. We get out of the canoe, stand in flowing water, and bash the ice dam with our paddles. "Not very elegant," John says, laughing. A lead opens up and what's left of the ice sluices through, as does our canoe. We jump back in. Ice shelves are cantilevered over the water. Beneath are rows of icicles, fingers testing the water. Warm or cold?

Every change in temperature causes incalculable disruptions. It can undo the connectedness between a species and its environment. Spring now occurs six to twenty-four days earlier, depending on the landscape, elevation, and latitude. On this Wyoming river, warming has led to reduced summer stream flows, with dire consequences for fish populations, as well as for birds and animals dependent on them. The early onset of spring throws breeding, nesting, and birthing cycles off and the migration patterns of insects, birds, plants, and animals into turmoil. Grass and flowers come earlier but dry up sooner, altering the availability of food.

A muskrat swims in front of us, pushing a pile of sun-cured grass. Nearby, a beaver's domed house is buried in snow. Muskrats often live inside or right next to beaver dens. While a beaver's house is lodged in ice with a vent hole at the top, muskrats build flimsier shelters. They use the beaver's dammed-up water for ingress and egress, swimming out underwater to forage for food at the bottom of the pond.

A muskrat's dive lasts only forty seconds. To hold her breath even that long, she must store extra oxygen in her blood and muscles—an ability that increases by 42 percent in winter, since food is less abundant and it takes longer to get back to the breathing hole from under the ice. Same thing goes for beavers, and in the Arctic, for seals, whales, and walruses.

Now goldeneyes, bufflehead, mallards, and mergansers fly ahead of us, joining the swans and geese. Exposed willow roots hold spans of candle ice, long crystals bunched together in bouquets. A snow squall lofts by, like a sail filling with wind. Ice pans snap. A beaver tail slaps. It's percussion, not current, that's carrying us downstream.

Like two separate thoughts running simultaneously, a mink works the margins of the river, while a coyote traverses the snowbank above. A bald eagle cocks its head at who-knows-what on the too-white page of the pasture. We paddle, but it's the river that's taking us. We drink in her sounds. The Inuit in Greenland thought that fog was born when a thirsty woman drank a whole river and spit it out as mist.

Ice at river's edge is jagged, serrated like a knife. Whom does it cut? What has been sliced away? Earlier the radio carried war news. Hasn't there been enough violence right here with life ending, life beginning between every breath?

Banked snow stretches in ribbony stripes that are sway-backed and bending. One beaver swims out from under willow branches, then another and another. Soon there's a whole line of them swimming in an *S*-shaped formation in front of the canoe. Are they trying to slow us down or lead us away? One thing is clear: they are in charge of river traffic, and we travel by their rules.

Above a hidden side channel, a cow moose and last year's

calf stand knee-deep in snow. When we pass, they charge down into the water, then run back up. Under a cold sun beaver slides glisten. A swan's nest rests on top of a domed lodge. A cut bank, so steep that snow will not stay on it, is a brown wall that bends us sideways. We pick up more geese as we go. There are now twelve pairs, plus all kinds of ducks. We portage over another ice dam, and where the river thins, mirrored mountains grind to nothingness. As water deepens, pieces of ice float with us—a company of geometric oddities—triangles, parallelograms, rhomboids. Midriver, they are snagged by a huge willow root like LP records stacked up against a twisted spindle.

The river widens and tiny streams leak in. John narrates local history and points out where a stranger who corralled his horse for the night was found shot to death in the morning. He shows me the place where Tom Horn hid. "There was a saloon on that bank," he says, "and a store, a schoolhouse, and a log cabin with laundry flapping. Shoshone Indians floated this stretch, but never this early in the year. They would have used it only during summer hunts. The reason white trappers called this the Spanish River was because it flowed into a part of the country owned by Spain."

Mornings, the ice pans *are* the river; afternoons, the river is sun, its smooth skin disturbed by intruding gravel bars. We look for the wolves but see none. Late in the day, clouds slide in front of the sun and a light breeze wrinkles the water. Snow begins to fall. It alights on pieces of floating ice and melts quickly as more takes its place. "Just like us," John says quietly. "We haven't been here long, and we'll soon be gone." In falling snow the bow of the canoe goes white.

### 4

Home for the evening. Not lonely but alone. I think about what the river has shown me: the slinking mink, the tangled willow roots, the stain of sun on snow, and the *thonk, ping*, splash, and crack of its ice. Swans are white flowers floating. If this river were mine, I would call it the Unfastened, where scooped cutbanks shake winter free.

Just before dusk I strap on snowshoes and return to the river. Since tipping over the first day, I've longed for full immersion. On the bank, I take off one boot and stick my toe in. Instant pain. Try again, dipping the whole foot to the shin. I take off my clothes, step in, squat down, shoot back out of the water fast, get dressed, go home.

Dark comes. Black clouds blank out the ebbing moon. *Tcaxa'lxe'l* is a Navajo concept of darkness: sun cannot penetrate it; protection and invisibility are conferred by it; this darkness can move without making noise, which is why it can enter the body of anyone it likes and search their mind.

Early morning. Behind mist the sky whitens. Falling snow means the world is dissolving. A fragment of the horned moon breaks off in cloud. I step over the track of a wild swan.

5

John has been telling animal stories all morning—when and where he saw them, about the senseless killings of coyotes, swans, and wolves, and the blowing up of beaver dams. The story of the nervous moose was most unusual. While John was walking across a narrow bridge to the Carney ranch, a moose and her calf refused to move. She charged John; he leapt over the side of the bridge, hanging on to the edge. The moose stomped on his hands with her hooves, and he fell down ten feet onto the river ice. Stunned, he felt to see if his legs were broken. They weren't. Before he could stand up, something dropped right beside him. It was the moose and her calf. They'd both jumped off the bridge. "They fared poorly. Their necks were broken and they died right there next to me," he says.

We put in on the river near the place where the moose and the calf jumped to their deaths. Five tundra swans, three Canada geese, and two cinnamon teal fly up as we glide near the bridge. Farther along, a mother moose and her calf splash down into the water. "Will we be all right?" I ask. We drift nearer. Two coyotes chase each other across a stretch of snow. The moose lift their heads as we approach but ignore us. The animals from his stories keep appearing before us. "They must have heard you talking about them," I say. John smiles.

———

Where snow has pulled back, the ice has stretched to the breaking point and tiny beaches appear. A sandhill crane rests in a shaded cove. We see no muskrats and only one beaver slide, the impression etched into snow by its fat tail. An ice ledge breaks as we round a rock. "This is the section of water where the river bends so far back, it almost meets itself," John says. "We'll go an hour or so, and find that we're only a few feet away from where we began."

Oxbows slow time. They gnaw at rock and chew through land. They are a sinuosity trying to become a circle. Sometimes they succeed, sometimes not. It all depends on time, weather, and geology. Is a circle a line drawn around something, or is it center and edge, snowy island and river moat, massif and trail bound together? Unless we understand the nature of the circle, how all things are drawn together and flap with one wing, we cannot save the world or keep ourselves from destroying it.

Habitual thought and neurotic habits keep us bound up in our own airtight chambers with no sanity, no oxygen. But a circle keeps turning. "The return is important and different from the start," my monk friend said. But when and where does returning begin, if it's all just a circle?

Today our canoe drifts by. As if the hands on the clock needed to be greased. We defy time; we loop backward and forward

THE UNFASTENED: ON THE SPANISH RIVER

like a god, sweeping the hand of fate this way and that. In the process, things come in doubles: the same house occurs twice, and there are two of every bird and animal—coyotes, moose, swans, muskrats, ducks, beavers, and geese. Spilling snow, slowing time, throwing off riffles, the river is trying to remake itself as a whole world.

Downstream we encounter commercial traffic: muskrats pushing stacks of dried grass to a far bank. Behind us, beavers slap their tails, not applauding our passage but warning us to stay away. There's almost no ice now; we've dropped from eight thousand feet to seven thousand four hundred feet in altitude. Each hairpin turn holds a swan; each straightaway is home to a mink, a duck, or a squadron of beavers. Another turn and we glide back the way we came, but on a new piece of water. Here the river bends so sharply it is an elbow digging into its own back. A willow-studded island is almost halved.


Water seeking water, that's what we're seeing. It's nothing new. Like everything and everyone, the river is filled with longings, no matter that they come to nothing. No bitterness ensues. At least we have lived and died and lived again. Every bend is a kind of death. Not death's death, but the end of the instant, and the release of the riverscape before the next one comes.


The canoe bends hard to the left. We pass a pile of ice that is see-through rubble, reminding me that I no longer have to believe the contents of my mind. In the dirt of the south-facing bank a young willow is sprouting, but the other side is a white wall, its midriff sag a measure of how long winter has lasted and how close we are to spring. A frigid wind begins to blow; a snow cloud lifts up from a knot of mountains behind us; we are pressed forward into shadow, into turbulence. There is un-evenness everywhere and union within it.

The river keeps bending back and carving away. It is trying to show us what we know and how to move. More sandhill cranes fly in. Ahead, a lone duck dives down as if catching the river in its beak. At the point where the river comes closest to meeting itself, I can see the duck grabbing at things as if catching strands of water in its beak. He finds one, then another, and an-other, and pulls, until finally, the whole river comes straight and begins its long southward journey.

*Part Four*

# HOW MEMORY ENDS AND BEGINS

*. . . the right journey*
*is motionless; as the sea moves round an island*
*that appears to be moving, love moves round the heart—*

—DEREK WALCOTT

# MARCH. WINTER'S END

Rough and fresh. That's how the day felt as it began and ended. Just another one the meadowlark blew into being, Gary says. A meadowlark has been singing on a post near his barn. I am in Montana again. There has been almost no snow all winter, and spring has arrived with blustery rain that alternates with hot sun. A scent blows our way, signaling the new season, but the source of the spring sweetness eludes us. We drive north and east to the foot of the Garnets, then the Rocky Mountains, to find where the scent is coming from.

Where the Blackfoot River bends double, we get out and walk. A flicker is knocking itself out on a leafless cottonwood tree. On a pond-dotted plain encircled by high mountains, we come upon sandhill cranes, as well as Canada geese, snow geese, and mergansers. The ground is damp. A few miles away, farmers have begun to plow. I wonder how many ground-nesting birds are lost to machinery each year. Our urge to undo things must come from an idea that what we find in the natural world isn't good enough, that our tinkering will make it better. Spare us the scandal of improvement, I say.

The cranes hop and flap—intimations and warm-ups for their mating dance. Then they settle down to look for food. Picking up cow pies in their beaks, they shake out the bugs. Just up the road is Glacier National Park, a place that is about to lose all its glaciers. The big ones are only a third the size they were in 1850, and the smaller ones have disappeared altogether. The total area covered by glaciers has declined more than 75 percent, and the temperatures have risen almost 2 degrees.

High mountain biota, trapped in the last cool refuge possible—at the tops of these peaks—are in rapid decline. Populations of pika and marmots are disappearing, lower elevation plants and animals are intruding on high alpine aeries. Cold-loving plants and animals have nowhere else to go. It's predicted that just a 3 percent rise in temperature will destroy 80 percent of alpine island habitats. I try to readjust my eyes so I can see what goes missing.

The ten warmest years have occurred in the last ten years. The summers have been scorchers, with months of hundred-degree days. When the Bush administration excised a long section on climate change from the 2003 EPA report, a *New York Times* ad ran with the caption GEORGE BUSH COOKS THE BOOKS ON GLOBAL WARMING. Now he's doing what he can to have seventy-five thousand natural-gas wells drilled on a mesa forty miles from my Wyoming cabin.

———

Some days it seems there is no basis for reality. We are unanchored and have no sacred alignment with life. The gas wells are going into the middle of an antelope migration corridor. We wonder why we feel lost. Too many of us are "merchant class," all about buying and selling. Our intimacies have been given up, not just with one another but also with the billion, trillion elements of life in motion around us, a cyclical spectacle always showing a new facet of its permanent changeability.

Too often our only consort is ego, but even she is a mystery and, willy-nilly, we let her have her way. Often, we are afraid of prolonged intimacy with any one subject, person, or place, for fear that we'll see too much and lose our capacity to tell winners from losers, or have to forfeit our "permission" to kill whatever gets in our way: weeds, fish, lovers, friends, foes, insects, solutions, and animals.

We no longer sing landscapes into being as the northern Maidu once did, or cause bits of floating earth to be stitched together with deer sinew. We bring on droughts because our rain is ineffectual. It falls on ground that is overgrazed, fallow, plowed up, burned off, or paved over. We only destroy. We are serial killers, the Harvard biologist E. O. Wilson reminds us.

Over lunch another biologist, George Schaller, tells me that it's not population that concerns him at the moment, but greed. We want so much, and so much is foisted upon us. We don't go outside often enough to experience the natural fecundity inside ourselves or of the world.

In twenty years there will be no glaciers on the planet. Lodgepole pine and western cedar will give way to hemlock and spruce, and these in turn will invade alpine meadows where elk like to graze. The forest fires that have ravaged the Yellowstone ecosystem this summer have reduced the white bark pine that is an important food source for grizzlies. The warming of streams is causing cold-water trout to move upward in altitude, but that climb can bring on early ice that may kill them.

In the meantime, the forest fires send eroded soil into the rivers; bumblebees and other alpine-flower pollinators are confused by smoke. A warmer world is an unhealthy world. Funguses, rusts, and insects are moving in and killing some species of frogs, trees, and butterflies. Virulent viruses are killing domesticated animals and people.

In Switzerland, a botanical garden that has specialized in tropical plants for fifty years recently lost a tree. When one of the botanists went on a hike in the foothills of the Alps, he discovered a palm tree growing. "A palm tree in Switzerland," he lamented. "And some still say there's no global warming."

Sun glistens. Gary and I savor the last vestige of cold. Snow on the north-facing roof of the cabin slides, then stops, freezing into what looks like a wave. Icicles, what in Japan's "snow country" dialect are called *dagi*, hang from it. In 1835, a few years after Charles Darwin toured the southern Andes by boat and horseback, Suzuki Bokushi wrote *Snow Country Tales*.

Bokushi lived in the heart of the Japanese Alps and tells of being buried in snow for eight months of every year. When a villager began measuring snow, it averaged 185 feet, often more. The snow was wet and heavy. Walkways were cut with wooden shovels between thatched-roof farmhouses. It was necessary to dig them out every day, lest they become entirely buried. Blinds woven from miscanthus reeds hung from the eaves to keep blowing snow off covered verandas. The people lived in darkness. Oil lamps had to be lit all day. They walked through snow tunnels between villages and towns. The word *mabu* connoted not only a dark tunnel, but also a woman's secret love affair.

Bokushi wrote: "When it finally stops and enough can be dug away so that a tiny window can at last be opened—then oh! The brightness that greets our eyes makes us feel as if we were suddenly born into a shining Buddha world!"

The culture of the Japanese Alps was cold-adapted. For heavy loads, they used long sleds called *shura; kajiki* were snowshoes made from the twigs of the jagara tree; snow vests were made from tree bark; snow boots, shoes, and leggings were all made out of straw. Long poles that measured snow depth were used to calculate how much tax should be imposed on the residents each year. When people went to the mountains, they had to use special, honorific words to appease the gods, the *kamisama*. Up there, a straw raincoat was *yachi*, sedge hats were *tetsuka*, a person dying was *magatta*, and a woman's sex organ was referred to as a "bear's den."

A yearly bacchanalian event called hall-pushing took place in a temple where men and women first disrobed, then, on command, all began pushing a wall. Naked and sweating, the participants were so tightly packed that their breath became the local weather. "The exhalation of this multitude is like smoke or fog. It dims the sacred torches and rises up to the roof, where it condenses and falls like rain; the steam pouring out of the open peaks of the gables billows into the sky like a cloud."

Now the ceremony of hall-pushing has been replaced by climate-forcing. Instead of releasing steam from naked bodies in spiritual pursuit, we are pushing against the temple walls of *sila*—the great power of nature and weather—with our "democracy of gratification" and its industrial wastes: heat-trapping greenhouse gases and aerosols; black carbon (soot) from the incomplete combustion of fossil fuels and biomass burning, which absorbs sunlight and heats the atmosphere, melts ice sheets, and causes a dangerous rise in sea level.

On the wall I've tacked a newspaper photo of a bird singing, maybe a meadowlark. Its breath is visible, white wafting up into the cold air, but I can only think about black. Soot, that is, and smoke, and oil.

Gary and I lay out bits of food on the table, feeding each other like two birds. Later we walk in the dark, following a tiny stream through aspens and willows. For a time our legs pump together as if driven by the same pistons. We don't speak, but our skulls crack open like ripe fruit. Is this all there is to tenderness? Yes. And the way winter comes down piecemeal, one snowflake at a time, followed by spring.

The moon rises. The moon is a circle, full in all its phases—

full, half, new, dark. I search the ground and see where a single snowflake has fallen and melted; now, it's a thumbnail lake wedged between two stones. Ice teaches water about cold, but there is no ice without water. And no matter how small its pools, the moon still shines in them.

We lie on our backs in Gary's dark room. It's just a shed, really, with no running water and a shit bucket in the back, and he's touchy about anyone being there. Rain begins. We light a fire. The coming of warmth is like thought attaching itself to form. There are these little acts of creation going on all the time, but so often they pass by ignored.

We lie still. Holding each other makes the endorphins flow. A cracked window lets in the scent of rain. The small room becomes a place like spring itself—where emptiness fills up, where memory begins.

# Part Five

# A THOUSAND-MILE
# SAILING TRIP TO SPITSBERGEN

# ROUGH WATER

May 26. Left Tromsö, Norway, this evening at a time when in London it would be getting dark, but where we're going it will be light all night. When the mainsail is hoisted the boat lists to starboard and halyards slap the mast. Six sails go up. A hard westerly wind fills them. I'm on a Dutch boat painted red, called the *Noorderlicht*—meaning "northern lights." It's a 150-foot steel-hulled, gaff-rigged schooner built in 1910, and we're traveling to the Arctic archipelago of Spitsbergen.

Light all afternoon, all night. The seas grow heavier. We pass the last Norwegian lighthouse perched on a point of rock, then plunge north into the wild Barents Sea. The lighthouse stands for human memory. As we pull away from it, the schooner is lost and memory is gone. The sea is the hypnotic present that exists behind thought; ahead, the ocean is dented and glinting. Now I know what I love about land: the *firma* part of *terra* exists to exert calm. As soon as we leave it, the sea heaves up as if trying to excise from its skin this boat, this steel splinter.

We are alone on the water, a crowd of twenty strangers— scientists, naturalists, painters, writers, sculptors, photogra-

phers, a sound artist, and two film crews—going to the far
north to see these arctic islands and better understand the dy-
namics of the North Atlantic Drift and climate change in a
northern ecosystem.

The Arctic Ocean, toward which we're headed, is 54,000
square miles of sloshing ice, a reservoir of cold at the top of
this hot-box planet. Hung from its permanent ice are the islands of Spitsbergen (Svalbard), Franz Josef Land, Severnaya
Zemlya, Novo Sibirskie Ostrova, Wrangel, Axel Heiberg, Ellesmere, and Greenland. The ocean is, itself, an island of ice over
which a semipermanent low-pressure system swirls.

The Arctic is punctured by poles: the fixed North Pole at
90 degrees north, a drifting Magnetic North Pole, and a Geo-
magnetic North Pole, which is the tip of the earth's magnetic
axis, located just west of Qaanaaq, Greenland. In the 1920s
Australian explorer Sir Hubert Wilkins, who tried to write the
history of weather, flew to the point of ice in the Arctic Ocean
most distant from land—eleven hundred kilometers. The Arctic is a canary giving warnings about the health of the planet.
Its ills are a symptom that points to root causes of every
ecosystem's illness.

A decade ago I sailed the inland waterways of southeast
Alaska with Brendan Kelly, an arctic-seal biologist who had
spent twenty years doing fieldwork on the ice. When I talked
to him recently, he said, "Climate is what we all talk about now,
because the ice is going fast and whatever oscillation we im-
pose on the computer models, the same linear signal shows up.
That signal is the one made by automobiles and industry—

human-caused pollution—and it's very strong. This warming trend is a frightening thing. As the albedo effect—the ability of ice and snow to deflect solar heat back into space—decreases, things get warmer. More solar heat is absorbed, and the increase in temperatures grows exponentially. Which means we lose more and more ice."

He continues. "The history of climate is cyclic and fluctuating. It's hard to superimpose an indicator like human-caused pollution when there is no analogue to draw from. There has been no other time in the history of the world when greenhouse gases, airborne methane and mercury, desertification and deforestation have been around. Now we have to put the fluctuating signals of climate against the nonfluctuating one of anthropogenic changes. The trouble is we don't know exactly what we'll get. And there's no place in the world where we see atmosphere, oceanic, and ecosystem changes more dramatically than in the Arctic. It's called 'the polar amplification effect.' We could lose more than half the sea-ice cover in two decades or faster. When climate changes too fast, extinctions happen. We better begin to think of how we're going to save ourselves."

House-sized swells lift up. The Dutch crew of three—Ted, Maaike, and Ward—plus a cook, Anna, are hardy and efficient. Maaike's "five-kilo dog," Isbrun, runs the decks until it gets too rough, then retreats to the captain's quarters below. His name means "burning ice," a reference to arctic legends of an earlier time when animals could talk and understand what humans said and ice burned to give heat and light.

Nothing is burning tonight. Instead, we have gray skies, persistent rain, and ocean swells that lap the sides of the *Noorderlicht* like cold flames. This voyage, called the Cape Farewell Expedition, is the brainchild of David Buckland, a British photographer and sailor with a penchant for science. Four years ago David announced that he wanted to go sailing in the Arctic. What he refers to as his "selfish" dream changed into one that will make a contribution to society. The voyage will be used as a narrative tool to explore marine biology, oceanography, geography, ecology, and the arts in an interactive program for schools in the United Kingdom.

Because the crew is so small, we all help on deck according to our abilities. Round-the-clock watches are assigned; mine is from midnight until three. On deck I'm given a harness and clip into the rail near the wheel. Rain turns to sleet, then rain again. We can see because it is light, but we can't stand: the decks are covered in ice. With the starboard rail almost under water, one slip and anyone could go overboard. Who would see?

Below, the misery of seasickness begins to take hold. It's more than rough; fifteen-foot swells break against the forward rail. Midway through my watch, Maaike brings a slice of rye crisp spread with jam. "Better to have something in your stomach," she says. The rigging creaks and the *Noorderlicht* shivers. Still jet-lagged, I feel my equilibrium unravel. As soon as I go below to lie in my bunk, I'm sick too. Oh, misery . . .

———

Once there was a Penobscot Indian (in Maine) who was taking care of his sick wife and dreamed that "the ground suddenly began to heave like a wave, rising and falling round and round near where the sick one lay." He saw a bird flying under the ground. As soon as the bird was discovered, it came up from beneath the earth and died. After, the ground stopped heaving and the man's wife regained her health.

I search for the bird under this boat, but it will not reveal itself. Great black-backed gulls fly by, darting in and out of the concavities of the sails. The first night merges into the second day, and we're still under way, still wave-tossed, still heeling over hard in an eighteen-knot wind. But the crew is happy: we're doing what Ward, the second mate, calls a "natural nine": nine knots under sail.

May 28. Too sick to write. Watery buildings are falling on me. The deck jumps. The floor slides. We're living at a steep angle that I can't get used to. No one can walk, sick or not. A bench slides across the cabin and hits my shins. The film director and his fourteen-year-old son, Liam, take turns vomiting in a pail. Casper, a brainy journalist, runs to the rail. Maaike comes through with more rye crisp and suppositories. "What are those?" Nick, a cameraman and watercolorist, asks.

"They're for seasickness. You stick them up your bum."

He looks shocked. "My bum?"

Maaike smiles, puts one in his hand, and walks away.

Gary Hume, a painter from London, staggers through. I ask why he looks so well, and he says jauntily, "Oh, I just spit up like a cat when I need to [he makes a small cackling noise], then I get on with what I'm doing."

I'm less lucky and sit cross-legged on the saloon's banquette shaking with cold. I doze this way, "like a little blond Buddha," someone says. Once, when I open my eyes, I see Phil, one of the cameramen, sliding across the floor on his knees, elbows shoving the plastic bucket toward someone who needs it. Jamaican by birth, Phil was an ordained Catholic priest who requested dispensation from the pope to be released from his vows. But his sense of service is still intact; he's always helping, making us laugh, busing dishes for the cook, offering kindness laced with humor to everyone.

What time is it? Rain has not stopped. Gray light smears itself over a gray ocean. Gary Hume is at the helm, then Ward, then Ted, David, and Carolyn, a friend of the Cape Farewell project who has come to help sail. I can see but I don't want to. No one eats, no one talks. A few years ago a friend, Bill Hunter, who was sailing solo from Hawaii to California was lost at sea during a bad storm. Fifty-foot-high waves dismasted his small boat. He set off his EPIRB—an emergency location signal— but the coast guard couldn't make the rescue because the waves were too big. Bill must have gone below and closed the hatch— it's possible to survive this way no matter how many times the boat rolls—but when the helicopter returned the next morning the hatch had broken apart and Bill was gone.

There are times now when I wonder if we'll ever get to

land. Or will we have to sail on rough seas forever? Up on deck something is banging hard, but I can't see what it is. There's only rain and a circle of gray seawater. The boat lifts and plunges, slicing waves and lurching into troughs like a horse that goes halfway over a fence then drops dead midair. I don't want a sea burial. Can I have something on demand at least once? (I know the answer, but never mind.) I want a complete absence of movement; I want land.

May 29. Midnight. Only a circle and nothing else. I sip "ship's broth" made by the captain. Wind comes out of the north—the direction we're going in—and the sails are taken down. This boat is too big to tack all the way to Spitsbergen. "In a while they'll shift around to the northeast," Ted, the captain, says quietly. He's all angles and bones, as if wind had sheared everything unnecessary from his eyes and face. We drink ginger tea and watch long-tailed skuas fly low through gaping troughs. "Ahhhh, my favorite bird," says Ko, almost purring as he stands beside me on the rail. He's a tall, bearded Dutch naturalist who looks Russian. Like us, the skuas are migrating north, except they'll get there long before we will.

Ted hardly speaks at all. He just squints, keeping his eyes on the gimbal-steadied compass and the uneven water ahead. A graduate of architecture school, he once worked for a year in an office but hated it. "A friend and I saw this boat. We quit our jobs that afternoon, bought it, and here I am."

———

The sea is a universe, albeit one whose superstrings have been chopped up. "It looks like *une grande salade*," Gautier, the French photographer, says. His Leica swings from his neck like a black timepiece. But here there is no time, and no photographer's "opportune moments of revelation." Nor is there any land. It's been gone from sight for three days. Only the sea and the *bardo* of the sea: no reference points, no rescue.

9:00 a.m. The *Noorderlicht* heads up into the wind. On Ted's command we hoist the sails because the wind has shifted over to the northeast as he predicted. The process takes half an hour—no America's Cup grinders on this baby. The temperature has been holding at 38 degrees Fahrenheit but now drops to zero. Rain continues and the decks are ice. Clipped in, I step up to the wheel. The boat plunges and I fall. Pain radiates from my lower back, and ludicrously, my foot gets caught in the spokes of the big wheel. David, who is at the helm, looks down: "Hmm. It's a bit difficult to steer this way," he says, laughing. I'm laughing too as he extracts my foot, but my tailbone is bruised. "Should have kept your tail on," he quips.

We've sailed together before but not on the open seas of the North Atlantic. A wave the size of a warehouse crashes over the bow. David grins. Fourteen years ago, when a virus attacked his heart and he had nine cardiac arrests, his first thought in the recovery room was: "I want to sail."

Maaike brings tea and cookies from the lower depths of the galley, a part of the boat I haven't been able to go to for days. She and David check the chart and make a GPS reading. A rough spot capsizes the teacups. "That could be us," Albert, the soundman from Guyana, says. He's more than green at the gills.

"It's always like this on the Barents Sea," Maaike says. "We call it the Devil's Dance Floor."

The island-born explorer Willem Barents gave these islands the name Spitsbergen because of the pointed mountains he saw as he sailed this coast in 1594. The Dutch were desperately searching for a northwest passage to avoid the Spanish-ruled seas of South America and Cape Horn, and to gain supremacy over the British in the northern oceans.

Barents captained the *Mercurius* in 1594 and made it to latitude 77 degrees north. Another trip was organized in 1596 when a group of Dutch merchants offered a reward to anyone discovering the northwest passage. Two ships went out, and Barents was on one of them. From Bear Island they sailed north but were blocked by ice. Barents persuaded Captain Jacob van Heemskerck to sail east around the tip of the Russian island, Novaya Zemlya. "We came upon a great heap of ice that we could not sail through it," he wrote in the ship's journal.

It was September and the ice came in fast, crushing the ship. The crew built a driftwood house on the island with "sea-wrack for the roof and chinking of the walls." They cooked polar bear meat over a central fire but suffered from scurvy. For entertainment, they built a "golf course" between the hut and the crushed boat.

During the winter, bears took over the ship. In the middle of March the sea began to open. On June 13 Barents and his crew went off in open boats—converted from rowboats—"to get out of that wilde desart, irksome, fearfull, and cold countrey." As they passed Icy Cape at latitude 75 degrees north, Barents, who was very ill, asked to be lifted up so he could see the great promontory. They did so. Afterward he examined a chart, asked for a drink of water, and promptly died. It was June 20.

The survivors sailed on without their captain and were rescued by Russian fishermen, who nursed them back to health. The starving men were taken to the coast of Lapland. One of them wrote: "Wee saw some tress on the river side, which comforted us and made us glad, as if wee had then come into a new world."

# BEAR ISLAND

Up on deck I see life: barnacle geese fly by, and white-beaked dolphins leap straight up out of the water. The seas calm to a roll. "The ocean is no longer fighting us. Now she is just breathing," Ko says with a smiling solemnity. Isbrun, the dog, is in Ted's arms, shaking with excitement because he can smell and hear the whales before we can. Two humpbacks lumber by, their notched tails flicking water sparks through the air. Dolphins dive in our bow wave.

Ted turns the boat in a wide circle and cuts the engines. We wait. The whales reappear; whale-play goes on for half an hour. We roll from side to side; the whales undulate as if causing the seas to move. They can dive and stay under for an hour, storing huge amounts of oxygen in their blood. "Just like the people in the Andes who have 20 percent more hemoglobin than lowlanders," Ko says, grinning. "Humpbacks don't need to adapt to the cold. They're already insulated."

Kittiwakes wheel overhead, dipping into billowing sails and out again. The sun isn't shining, but the rain has stopped and the sky has brightened. Isbrun runs from porthole to porthole. "She's a whale hound," Maaike says. Sick as I've been, I can't suppress a big grin. Three days have passed. I'm not sure if it's afternoon or morning, but I'm optimistic: climbing the latitudes is like climbing a ladder: the farther north we go, the better the weather. After all, the Arctic is a polar desert even if we are at sea.

I'm shocked to find out that it's near midnight. We're under way and Maaike is at the helm. She is good-natured, small but strong. I ask her how she started sailing. "I was born on a houseboat and it went from there," she says briskly. Brunnich's guillemots fly by, moving much faster than we are. Is this a race? No answer. Something grabs Maaike's attention. In the distance a white bubble appears on the horizon. "It's land," she says. "Bjornoya. Bear Island."

Latitude 74.5 degrees north. An island slowly comes into being, the same one Willem Barents sailed from before he died at sea. It is rimmed with ice, swathed by clouds, and ends in purple cliffs where seabirds nest and fledge. A line of ducks flies, a black line against a gold sky. Everything here is made of lines, all skewed, broken-arrowed, picking up bright lights and cool hues as they travel. A cloud in the northwest throws snow into the sea. As we approach the west side, sunlight breaks on cliffs. Strips of green lie curled between amphitheaters of rock. We swing around and start up the east side. Here the land slumps from a taut ridge. Lobes unfold, making giant steps down to the sea.

Between the iceberg and the island a slow swell moves west,

sinking under our weight, then lifting up again, carrying sea-gulls and evening light. Brash ice, jammed against the foot of the island, clinches it tight. A wide collar of ice extends far out to sea. We've come here to anchor for the night, but there's more ice than we had anticipated. Ted checks the depth finder to see if it's shallow enough to drop anchor. He shakes his head, no. That means another thirty hours of sailing in rough seas.

For the time being we relish the calm. Seasickness ends. As we motor to the lee side of Bjornoya, a trance comes over us. Small swells lift and drop the mat of sea ice and our boat with it. There's a symphony playing: the sound of sloshing ice-chimes and sluicing meltwater. It's May. We're at latitude 74.5 degrees north.


"Bear!" Maaike shouts. We look: a polar bear is running across the ice. He leaps from floe to floe, swims the crevasses, leaps again. Now he jumps down onto the beach and swats at an eider duck caught between two pieces of ice but misses. Looks all over for it. Gives up. Strides away. As he jumps from the beach onto the land, his movements are elastic and effortless. He stands and, nose up, catches our scent. What are we? The human perfume is too alluring; he slides into the water and swims toward the *Noorderlicht*.

Are we dinner or trouble? Bears are no longer hunted here, so he's fearless. He sniffs and swims, sniffs again and moves closer, his nose a black seed drifting to us. Near the boat's stern he treads water and takes a good look at our mob hanging over the rail. The mixed scents of diesel, humans, and cooked food must be confusing. He turns in a small circle. We're inedible after all. He swims back to shore.

Polar bears can get hurt on both ends of the climate spectrum because their main food is seals. Too much ice and they can't get at the seals; too little ice, same story. Seals have their own problems with declining ice. They give birth to their pups and nurse them on ice ledges just under the snow. If the ice thins too much, the ledges don't hold; as snow cover decreases, the pups are exposed to predation by birds as well as foxes and bears. If seal populations decline, bears starve; if the ice thins or melts altogether, seals die.

As warming increases, freeze-up comes later in the fall. Bears starve simply waiting for the ice to come in, because they stalk their prey using ice as both a platform from which to see and a blind behind which to hide. Without ice, polar bears can't catch seals.

The *Noorderlicht* jostles in ice. I think of Osip Mandelstam's marvelous title *The Noise of Time*. Up here, time is an undifferentiated, oozing mat of ice. There is no diurnal sequence, but all light, all night, all day, ticking away until September.

I feel broken, full of dread: another thirty hours under way in rough seas, another night of seasickness. We motor slowly away. Mist warps the upper reaches of Bear Island. Snow falls.

For a long time I glass the bear with binoculars. It's the middle of the night, and the air is cool. There's a sun, but instead of setting, it is suspended at half-mast and shines down on the edge of the world, pooling its light in water. The half-opened lid of a gray cloud is the sun's eye; the pupil is gold.

The bear is gone. He wandered back into the white folds of the island. Where land ends, ice reaches a long arm out to us as if hanging on to the horizon's silver bar. Swells surge by pushing us west. We motor past a shaft of rock that sticks out of the water. Knife or feather? Wraparound clouds go, new snow falls, little auks fly, smooth-skinned water goes glassy, then breaks into a tornado of swirling gulls.

If global warming persists, all this will be gone. With no ice, the Arctic ecosystem vanishes: bears, walrus, seals, seabirds, fish. I look back; the ice collar holds tight and keeps the island from following us. Deep in its interior, the bear is a vanilla speck. At a nod from the captain, the mainsail goes up and the schooner sails, jibs flying.

# A BARRIER OF ICE

3:00 a.m. The *Noorderlicht* slaloms through splintered sea ice. Maaike stands on the bowsprit directing David, who is at the helm. He spins the wheel fast one way, then the other, his face red from exertion. Because the boat is so slow to respond, he has to anticipate which way to go a hundred yards ahead of actually turning. Icebergs, frazil ice, pancake ice, and curdled sea ice litter the water's surface. Ko is at the rail. "Isn't this beautiful?" he says, in a sea-song cadence that lifts and falls.

Ted takes the wheel. "Ice starts in the east and melts in the west," he says. We veer west, but no matter how far we go, the barrier of ice stays. Now we are heading straight for it and my heart sinks. Will this ice edge be impenetrable? Will we have to turn back and sail another five days in wild seas? Ted smiles, saying nothing. We creep forward on a collision course, then an opening appears. Ted spins the wheel hard to starboard. We slip through.

Sun is out. Before us is a new world: a plain of open and relatively calm seas. Ted corrects our course and turns north, while Val and Sara, the two oceanographers from

Southampton Oceanography Centre, take the temperature of the sea.

One of the ironies of global warming is that it may cause some places to get colder. The Gulf Stream is tropical water that flows north from Africa past western Europe and the United Kingdom, keeping that part of the world much warmer than it should be, considering its latitude. The Gulf Stream is part of a closed loop called the global thermohaline circulation system, and on the map it looks like a lopsided figure eight— the same one the migrating arctic birds take from north to south, the same one I've been following in my recent travels.

"This conveyor belt of warm water works like a swim-mer doing laps between poles," Val says. As soon as the warm water reaches the far north it is cooled as it mixes with the Polar Current. The water grows denser, bends under, sinks, does a flip, and begins flowing south, and around the loop goes. Now the warming climate is causing the Greenland Ice Sheet to melt, and billions of gallons of fresh water are pouring into the northern sea each year. The ice melt has increased by 16 percent since 1979, and in 2002 at least 264,400 square miles of ice was seen to be melting.

The *Noorderlicht* hovers over the current line between the Gulf Stream and the Polar Current. Val and Sara lift the two cylinders of seawater and haul them over the rail. Carefully, they measure water temperature and salinity. Val looks up from her computations, puzzled. "Even small changes can af-fect how the 'pump' operates," she says. "These water streams are not as clear-cut as the maps indicate. It's a bit of a jumble.

We're getting a lot of cold temperatures where there should be warm. This could mean that the meltwater from Greenland has already diluted the tropical Gulf Stream. If that's so, we may be in for a big change. Sea level will rise and Europe will turn frigid. It happened during the last ice age. That's why the Norse colonies failed. It got too cold to raise crops and hay. And it could happen again, quickly: I'm not talking about hundreds of years, only a few—five or ten. The brakes just go on and the conveyor belt stops. And it could stay that way for several centuries. Getting hotter can mean getting colder. It's all so fragile. What happens up here has repercussions all over the world."

The day started in ice and ends in sun. The wind freshens, sails go back up, and we're under way again. The "way" is much smoother this time. These are rolling seas instead of ones that rock. "Rock and roll" must have been a sailor's term, a nautical bump and grind.

Yesterday, in the rough water of the Barents Sea the *Noorderlicht* shivered, groaned, and banged. Now, with a following wind—a wind that is behind us—we sail at 8.6 knots in a soft forward rhythm as if paced to the human heartbeat. "Life is wind," Ward says.

More than half the incident sunlight is absorbed by the topmost foot of the sea. Ten meters down, all the colors in the visible spectrum are absorbed except for blue. Blue stays, after every other color drowns. The sea prefers blue. It drinks it down, then brings it back up when molecules backscatter light. Blue rises to the surface and dances, snakelike, then sneaks away, seeping into the atmosphere. Periwinkle everything, that's what I want. Or just blue. Why is sadness called the blues?

The upper cabin is crowded and everyone is busy. Val and Sara log in data on computers. Gautier, Liam, Garry Doyland, and Suba, two geography teachers, play Monopoly. Albert and Phil, both immigrants from the Caribbean Basin, talk about lost cultures. Out the port window a line of ruffled water reels by. "There aren't any big waves now because the ice is near," Ko says. "It is a wonderful force, the ice, is it not?"

I love my middle-of-the-night watch. The night sun casts an eerie light across the sea. Under us, streams of tropical water dance with the Polar Current, making a thick blue-green broth. Halyards *ping, thwack,* and vibrate. As we go north, it gets colder and drier. At 3:00 a.m. it's 26 degrees Fahrenheit, and the blaze on the water stretches a long way.

# HORNSUND FJORD

May 30. Where one day ended and another began I can't be sure. Much of the voyage has been sea-*bardo*, and I've been deeply lost in it. Sometime during my watch there was a solar eclipse, but no one could see it because there were clouds. "What's there to see?" Gary Hume asks tauntingly, and looks skyward. "Obscurity," says David Hinton, a BBC film director, in his Oxford-trained, world-weary way. "You mean the dark side of ourselves," Gary says, grinning catlike.

Storm-battered, we pass the ravaged torso of an iceberg. Wind waves splash on it, making it rock. A ray of sun knifes down. It's impossible to be depressed in this light. But one can be confused.

The compass needle swings giddily across the four cardinal points, unable to stop anywhere. The whole earth is a magnet. The electrical currents that simmer in the hot, liquid core vibrate up from magnetic rocks laid willy-nilly in the crust. The two are constantly interacting: the magnetic pole at both ends of the Earth drifts because the magnet reshapes the core's electric currents. These modify the electromagnet, which in turn modifies the currents, and around it goes. Every movement in nature evokes a response.

Hanging over the rail, we peer at waves perishing. They pitch up like breasts on the port side of the boat; on the starboard side they are green wind-walls slit open—wider than a nipple—that release white foam. For a short time a polar storm wraps darkness around the tops of the masts and drops snow. After-ward, sun shines doggedly, as if by rote.

The sea and the ear are connected. Each bump, tilt, and slide of the boat registers in the inner ear. *Labyrinth* is the word anatomists use: deep inside our heads are looping canals and a snail-like cochlea filled with a gelatinous mass, freckled with lime crystals, and lined with delicate hairs that give us hints about whether we're walking on the walls or not. My inner ear is sick, all the hairs mown down. I fall, get dizzy, fall again.

I think it's morning. The ocean's "sinister eternity" has been fumbling with the clock, so the alarm never goes off. Three hours of sleep a day isn't enough even with the extra serotonin spurting through our brains from all the light. I stand on deck. The flanks of gray sea inflate and collapse. *So much breathing everywhere.* Under full sail, we see ice ahead, and beyond, the coast of the southernmost island of the Spitsbergen archipelago.

The *Noorderlicht* follows a coastline of mist-dripping peaks and snowy valleys. The friction of the boat's movement churns ice back into water. Val and Sarah scoop buckets of seawater and bring them on deck, then look at its plankton under a microscope. Deep in this sea broth live masses of plankton—macro-, micro-, nano-, and now, the smallest of them all, picoplankton, which ranges between 0.2 and 2.0 microns across. That's one fiftieth to one five-hundredth the diameter of a human hair. "They're reckless little things," one of the oceanographers says. "They thrive on the kind of extreme that puts human endurance to shame."

Some *Archea*—the evolutionary branch of beings to which plankton belong—can live at temperatures of 235 degrees Fahrenheit. Some exist with no oxygen at all, while others like water that is five times saltier than any ocean. Their populations are diverse and robust at both poles. They reach concentrations of hundreds of thousands per milliliter of seawater and not only recycle organic matter back into plants but also absorb carbon and supply nutrients directly to larger organisms—a critical part of the microbial loop of which we are all a part, and a helpmate in arresting global warming. Perhaps only these beings will survive a superhot Earth.

# BLUE ICE AND BEARDED SEALS

An ice belt—a long peninsula of ice—comes unfastened. We glide through. A glaucous gull eyes me, then swoops across the blank canvas of the wind-filled sail as if trying to write something there. A glacier expels a blue leaf. A *V* of little auks leads us in.

This is Hornsund Fjord, the first big inlet since leaving Norway four days and nights ago. Wind stops, water is calm. We drop the sails and, under power, glide in close. Here the mountains are fluted and their knife-blade peaks tilt back as if bent by too much cold. Ko comes on deck at midmorning. His face has collapsed. When I ask how he is, he takes a deep breath, then says, "Not so good. I just had a call on the satellite phone. My brother and his wife were killed last night in a car accident."

Everyone who hears goes silent. The ocean expands. Oxygen disappears. I look into his eyes. "Then we must get you to an airport so you can go home," I say. He shakes his head. "I don't know yet. I don't know anything right now."

---

There's a story from the upper Yukon River in Alaska about early travelers called K'och'en or "cloud people." They made journeys to another dimension of time and space where everything is white, where the only season is winter, and conventional reality was reversed, requiring people to learn anew how to behave. As we motor toward the snout of the Hornbrn Glacier at the head of this fjord, I begin to feel we have entered such a place.

On either side of the boat there are wide sweeps of white. Earlier I watched seawater freeze and turn to ice in front of the boat. Now sun is a knotted fist and water burns, festering into a silver shield. A sliver of ice rams into a cove, stirs things up, and blows back to the icy body from which it came. In the distance, half domes of granite lord over narrow, snow-glutted valleys—high arctic versions of Yosemite. Ducks rest on open water. Rosy sandpipers chatter on a narrow gravel beach. It snows.

We search for safe haven. Is there such a thing? Isbrun dashes excitedly around the deck. Yes, he says, there is. Nick paints a watercolor of a terminal moraine embracing a mountain peak. Two eider ducks, newly arrived, swim close together like newlyweds. Standing behind Ted at the helm, Maaike rests her hand tenderly on his shoulder.

Ko hangs over the rail, sad and silent, his hands clasped; Isbrun slips between his legs with a joyful bark. He knows things before we do: a pod of beluga whales appears, their white backs flashing as they swim quickly away. The anchor is dropped. Calm water is the one thing I'll ask for.

At Maaike's urging, Ted impersonates a bearded seal, then

he blushes. "We'll see them here, and maybe hear them," Maaike says. We *putt-putt* into the heart of the fjord. As the hull splits ice pans in half, the inlet opens wide: mountain, valley, mountain, glacier, valley, mountain, glacier—white, white, white, white.

During the last ice age, these islands and waters were covered by glaciers and ice sheets that extended all the way to New York City. Now land is rebounding and a new landscape is coming into being.

We go ashore by Zodiac. After so many days at sea the ground is reeling, but terra firma—hummocky moss and soft shale—makes a lovely bed. Purple saxifrage is coming into bloom. It has wintergreen leaves that never wither. The arctic dryad's bowl-shaped flowers invite visiting bees. Inside the blossom the bees bask, eat, and get warm. Here and there bearded seals are hauled out on bits of ice. Their heads are rust-colored, their fur tarnished silver, their long whiskers frosted white. As a child I was cast in the role of the Littlest Mermaid in Hans Christian Andersen's play. My legs and feet were bound tightly together in a narrow, iridescent skirt that ended in flippers.

The bearded seals' front flippers look like hands; the ones in back are knotted together almost playfully. It doesn't take much to see how in the semistarved minds of Inuit hunters, the merging and marriage of seals and humans could occur.

I'm curled up on a rock with water and ice lapping all around, while a snow bunting serenades me. Heard so often in my years in northern Greenland, it is utterly welcoming—a call home.

Dinner. French wine is uncorked and beer is downed to go with a hearty Dutch stew. We relax into a conviviality that goes on until 4:00 a.m. After the dishes are done, Anna, the cook, climbs the stairs from the galley with a wicked grin on her face, as Albert and Phil let loose with Caribbean rhythms. Maaike holds Isbrun on her lap. Colin plays a traveler's guitar and sings; Anna plays at seduction. We shimmy, stomp, laugh, and slither, as if mocking the wild ride we just had on the Barents Sea. Sometime in the wee hours, utterly drunk, Gary Hume grabs the shy captain and leads him in a faltering rendition of a waltz.

Out on deck, Max Eastley, a sound artist, drops a hydrophone over the rail and puts the headphones to my ears. Max is small and quiet, with soul-searching eyes and big ears. What I hear is astonishing. A fluttering whistle starts high and falls slowly down; it is the mating song of the male bearded seal, heard only in April and May. The whistles ululate. As one song ends, another begins—like a round—leaf upon leaf of sound.

We look from one side of the boat to the other. There are no bearded seals in sight. "They're somewhere," Ko says. "Maybe a mile or two from here. Water radiates sound long distances."

These are the watery calls of longing, a complex frequency that is wavering, fragile, doomed, eerie, and beautiful. "Like all love calls," Gautier says. What is it that lifts the notes after they fall? I wonder. Love and loss and more love—don't they always happen in the same kind of rushing slowness and arching falls?

Max traipses back and forth on deck all night recording seals. He wears his wool cap pressed down so that the tops of his ears are exposed and bent forward. "I can hear more this way," he says. The shapes within the human ear are musical instruments just waiting to be filled with sound. There are bugles, drums, tubas, French horns, and harps. Sound spirals through the auricle, strikes the tympanic membrane, and floods past the ossicles—the three bones of the middle ear—before entering the labyrinth, the deep north of the inner ear, where twenty thousand hairs of varying length are arranged like harp strings whose sole purpose tonight is to slap seal song against an auditory nerve, which, in turn, shoots those pulsations to the brain. At that moment, *we hear.*

Once, long ago, in southwestern Alaska, a female Yupik shaman put on a bearded seal mask. In an instant she fell through the floor and began to cry out. Her cries sounded exactly like those of a bearded seal. The sound made the onlookers feel as if their foreheads were opening up, they said. With the mask on, she was the seal.

We have no masks. But we have an ear for what is lyric. The ear is an eye. With it, we see our way to the end. Hearing is the last sense to go before death. In a coma once, I could hear

the doctor whispering to my mother on the other side of a
closed door, "I don't think she's going to make it." The vol-
ume in my brain was turned up crystal clear. My heart was
slowing to a stop, but I could hear theirs beating.

There are Inuit words in various dialects for "the bearded
seal who at this time of year is singing." In Anchorage I saw a
bearded seal mask at the museum; it was a head with a mouth
wide open as if singing, and its *yua*, the soul—another force—
was pushing through.


Near morning. We sleep on glass. It too induces a feeling of
falling because there are no rolling waves to keep us upright.
Under me, bearded seals dive deep to rake the benthic mud
with long whiskers for food. At this moment I'm anything but
lonely, and can no longer say "I" or "me." It is "us," all
twenty-four of us bound together by the rough passage we endured and the sudden beauty coming into our eyes and ears.

# BELLSUND AND VAN MIJENFJORDEN

June 1 and still snowing. Continental slosh and pancake ice spin as the tide comes in. An arctic fox track leads from a bird mountain to a puzzle of ice floes. As the ice shifts, the tracks disappear. A polar bear saunters across a snowy valley on all fours. "The ice bear is perhaps the loneliest of all the animals in the Arctic," Ko tells me. For no obvious reason, the bear stops, lays his head and shoulder on the snow, then rolls over with all four feet in the air.

We sail out of the storm into the sun and calm of Van Mijenfjorden. Ted and Maaike show us the marks on the chart that indicate how much the glaciers on these islands have retreated since they first sailed here ten years ago. A red line marks where they were; a blue line—where they are now—is much farther back.

Time in the Arctic beats to another clock. A caterpillar can take fourteen years to become a butterfly, freezing in middevelopment during the long winters, thawing out when summer temperatures rise, then freezing again. But once a caterpillar has reached maturity and becomes a butterfly, it lives only a few weeks, then dies of the cold that comes in August in these high latitudes. Arctic flowers, on the other hand, rush through their cycle—greening up, flowering, and going to seed in six weeks.

"I guess water has the longest life of all," Val says. "One drop melting out from a glacier can take a thousand years to go through the ocean's global circulation." David Hinton looks at her and grins: "One drop goes a long way."


Ko, Max, David Hinton, Albert, and I are taken by Zodiac to a thin ledge of rock that cantilevers out over the sea. We sit at the bottom of a vertical wall—a "bird rock." Albert and Max record; David, Ko, and I just watch. On the craggy face a city of nests rises. So many love stories up there: pair after pair of kittiwakes and Brunnich's guillemots are pushed close to-gether. It's like looking into the lit windows of a New York City apartment building at night. But the noise is much louder.

Kittiwakes make nests of mud and straw, but guillemots squat on bare rock. They don't bother making shelter. Their eggs are cone-shaped to take up less room. Because guillemots are stronger than gulls, they get better nesting sites. But once they've claimed their territory, there's nothing to do except sit and wait for the eggs to hatch.

We spy an arctic fox sneaking through the "bird suburbs," or, as I call them, the "birdbubs." Where barnacle geese are nesting, a fox leans around the edge of the wall trying to snatch an egg. A squawking bird-alarm sounds; the fox is attacked by glaucous gulls and quickly departs. In the aftermath, two kittiwakes fight over a female. The winner chases the other bird away.

Birds swirl and swarm. The noise intensifies. I close my eyes and listen, trying to separate out the thousands of overlapping cries: *kaka-week, kaka-week; kak-kak-kak-kak;* and the low *grrrr* of the Brunnich's guillemot. The air hums. The vibration of wings shatters complacency.

"I'm glad I'm here!" Ko yells. "To see these birds gives me hope when I am feeling there is none." A bird flies over with bits of grass hanging from its beak. Two kittiwakes groom each other using their necks like hands for fondling. One lifts off the nest, leaving its mate, who calls and calls: *ga . . . ga . . . ga . . .* Others return with food to share, or a bit of mud to shore up a sagging nest wall. Some couples just sit: face-to-face, neck-to-neck, beak-to-beak, utterly entranced with each other.

Far back, part of a frozen waterfall drops as if the noise had fractured the ice; birds cry out and flap up past it. On either side, wide sweeps of white bind fjord ice to sky.


Night. But light. On board the *Noorderlicht,* someone discovers that seal songs are traveling up the steel masts; this whole boat is a listening post, and we lean in to hear. The spiraling calls of the bearded seal are twisting down as if waves of water were bending waves of sound. *What are the uses of enchantment?* Dan Harvey, a sculptor, had asked earlier. Now I know.

Geological desire festers. Just north of here a line of sea vents spurt hot water into the Arctic Sea. The diastolic motion of the sea rocks me asleep, then awake. What is the difference between longing and loving? Perhaps this: longing is almost loving and surely losing; love is the constant inconstant, like a burning that is both instantaneous and light-years away.

I go below to rest. As soon as I put my head down, I hear love songs vibrating through the steel hull. My forehead opens and the seals' whistling cries pour in. Equilibrium is restored. In the deep north of the ear, the ampulla's sensory hairs sway to these songs.

In this way the ear combats loneliness: it's a shell with a wide entry, elaborate whorls, a pink auricle, and secret tracks that take up threads of song. Seabirds live in crowded colonies. Polar bears wander alone. Bearded seals live in loosely extended families. Longing is their common thread. Passion and solitude. That's all there is for us and all there is for the bearded seal.

A pale light slams against frozen windows. Even under way snow stacks up on deck. A nine-note snow bunting song sounds as we depart. We're taking Ko up the coast to the airport in Spitsbergen's only town, Longyearbyren, to catch a plane to Oslo, then Amsterdam. If all goes well, we'll arrive tomorrow. Behind us is a long spit of land, a thawing landscape on which we walked earlier, where the ground is corrugated solufluxion—all lobes and stones, the small ones separated out from the large ones in perfect polygonal mosaics.

Nature is the only true artist, and we are its apprentices. A piece of blue ice drifts by, ice from which all the oxygen has been squeezed out. I lean on the rail and breathe in. Blue ice is airless; the thing itself is total absorption: blue becoming blue, having been blue.

# TOXIC SPRING

There's so much extravagant beauty, and so much destruction and carelessness. What will the outcome be? A cloud bisects the mountain so that only the peak and foot show. An iceberg drifts by with a porthole through which we see more ice. At dinner, Gary Hume affects a strange Irish voice and manner. His comments are incisive and a little mean, which makes them wickedly funny. We laugh until tears come. "Watching the coast go by," he says, "is like three-dimensional walking standing still." We dance, letting the heaving deck throw us around. We can be quiet all together, and we can be loud.

Middle-of-the-night watch. The seas are running big. Our boat is a sieve. Water streams everywhere. Its holes are ears. If only we would listen. Life on earth is so robust that we haven't even begun to finish mapping the world's biodiversity. Yet we kill it off as it is discovered. Life goes the way of life: from the ice caps to the equator, from the Mariana Trench to the young, still-rising mountains, some sort of life can be found, and the internal complexities of the biosphere are only now becoming apparent.

No place looks as pristine as these islands, this sea, these fjords. The Arctic is a wide bowl, a basin that attracts water and atmosphere from the inhabited and industrialized nations to the south. Pollution from the United Kingdom, Europe, Russia, Eurasia, China, and the United States, as well as smoke and dust from Africa, Indonesia, and South America, find their way to the Arctic every day. Persistent organic pollutants, heavy metals, radioactivity, and petroleum hydrocarbons, plus smoke from fires and dust—what constitutes a global pool of contaminants—rides a round-the-world circuit of winds, ocean currents, and weather carrying the ills of so-called civilization to the top of the world.

In a paper titled "Physical Pathways of Contaminant Transport" I read grim messages. Westerly winds bring POPs, PCBs, heavy metals, pesticides (including DDT, which is still used in Asia, sold by the United States), and organochlorines from industrial Eurasia over the top of the North Pole that are washed by snow, fog, and rain from the air to the ground. Semivolatile compounds are transported by cycles of evaporation and condensation. Meltwater does the rest, feeding every stream, river, and lake in the arctic ecosystem. Slow-moving rivers can store pollutants in stream-bank sediments; fast-moving rivers move their dirty cargo seaward, causing estuaries and deltas to become particle traps.

Drift ice carries contaminants that sifted down from dirty air into the transpolar drift, spiraling into the Beaufort Gyre or the Labrador Current. Ocean currents slowly push water-soluable and particle-absorbed contaminants from distant industrial coasts into the Arctic Sea and out again down the East Greenland Current and through the Canadian archipelago. Sadly, the sea is the final resting place and sedimentary storage vault for pollution.

The Arctic is particularly toxic in spring. As snow begins melting, there's a chemical surge. The initial melt can remove as much as 40 to 80 percent of the total mass of the winter's accumulated airborne compounds. High levels of PCBs are found in the breast milk of Inuit women. The newest finding is the toxicity of flame retardants used in plastic casings, building materials, and fabrics. In polar bears, these endocrine disruptors are causing animals to "change sex," developing both male and female sex organs. A hermaphroditic bear was found on Spitsbergen in 1997, and others were found in Greenland, just a few hundred miles away.

Radionuclides have been high in the European Arctic since the 1986 explosion in Chernobyl. An American military plane that crashed off northwestern Greenland spread plutonium in Bylot Bay in 1968. A Cosmos-954 satellite spread radioactive material over Canada. Who knows what goes on at nuclear power plants? Arctic haze, actually smog, has intensified, and acid rain and snow are tallied up in the archives of glaciers.

Ironically, the Arctic's cold climate may be bacteria-resistant, but it attracts and preserves industrial pollution better than warm climates do.

Cycles and circles enclose us. They are all fixed paths, closed circuits, and we have to live with what we've created within them. Beauty and pollution ride the same trails. The aurora is beaded with lead and cadmium, snowbanks drift hard with heavy metals, rain is toxic, drift ice is radioactive, roaring rivers are pollution highways, the oceans are mercury sinks, the midnight-sun-filled days are cluttered with smoke and dust motes, and Earth and its atmosphere are becoming a hot cauldron where disease and contamination are stirred.

We are under sail; the horizon is a gray thread on which a few beads of ice are strung. Ocean currents clash. An iceberg is up-ended, sending shock waves to shore. "It's important to have hope," Dan Harvey says. "Despite the mess we've made. It means we have room for improvement. In my sculptures I work with grass. Grass teaches us hope. The way one blade can grow between the crack of a huge boulder." He shows me pictures of the floating fields of grass, grass bodies, grass books, and grass houses he's made. He transforms the ordinary and, like any arctic shaman, asks us to step into another way of seeing. Now he's making plaster impressions of ice. Looking out over the bay, he says: "Human eyes are cued to the color green because it has always meant food and water. But up here, the cue for hunters must have been white, or maybe blue. I've only been thinking in one season—summer. This vista of ice changes everything. I'll have to think in the hues of a new season."

A snowflake falls, moving the mass balance of a glacier from ablation to accumulation, but later it melts, sending the equation the other way. Every moment is teetering, and every glacier. Balance, then, must be imbalance: all tipping and tilting, gaining and losing, unending rock and roll. Nothing is steady. But that's okay. The boat's listing deck has taught us how to dance on rough seas, how to spin straight on steep angles, how to keep from falling once the water is still. Within us is what Emerson called "the soul of the whole," in which what is seen and the seer, what is heard and the listener, are one.

# LONGYEARBYREN

Latitude 78 degrees north. Tonight the horizon bends slightly. The world is not flat after all. As we enter Recherche Fjord, the ever-erudite Casper pays homage: "When to the sessions of sweet silent thought I summon up remembrance of things past." An eerie whistle catches our ears; the fjord is littered with drift ice, silver platters holding bearded seals.

We circle around and around, getting as close as possible. The seals' long whiskers glisten and their calls ride the air. We humans must be the most primitive beings on the planet, the most uncivilized. There is so much we don't hear, know, or sense in any way. I can't send my love songs through the water to anyone I love; I can't sing that way.

We idle beside one of the seals. He tolerates us for a long time, then slithers into his watery paradise. If the warming trend continues, the ice shelves where these seals raise their pups will melt and they will die.

On the way out of Bellsund Sound we spot another polar bear. Is the bear male or female, someone asks. Or both? Val says. When the ice goes, the bear goes. But she can't know that now. She steps from iceberg to iceberg, walks the length of a snowy valley, stops, looks up, yawns, and continues on her way.

Jason, an Australian diver, filmmaker, and North Pole guide whom we meet along the way, says, "Except for a few areas, the Spitsbergen islands have been beautifully preserved, but the committee forgot to include the ocean. The arctic ecosystem is very simple. It has three or four steps—from fish, to birds, to seals, to polar bears. Without a healthy sea, the arctic ecosystem collapses immediately. Bears, walrus, birds, and seals need fish. Fish need healthy water. They need to be left alone. At the moment the sea is being overfished. Take one element away and everything goes. How could the Norwegians be so shortsighted?"

The *Noorderlicht* sails down a coast wrapped in black smoke. Beyond are ramshackle wooden buildings and massive apartment blocks above on the hill. This is Barentsburg, a Russian coal mine and factory town. Spitsbergen has no indigenous population and is governed by an international consortium under the sovereignty of Norway. Fifty percent of the main island of Spitsbergen is contained in three national parks and two preserves for plant protection, but the rest of the island, including the area around Isfjorden, is a no-man's-land, with mining claims plus 250 claims within the national park boundaries. Barentsburg is one of them.

Ted asks if we want to visit. Some say yes, others no, but the yea-sayers win. Reluctantly I join the tour. The guide is self-appointed. He shows up at the dock and tells us it will cost twenty of whatever currency he's using. He's exuberant, having just arrived from Ukraine, where he made a fraction of the money he makes here. "And they fly us in a helicopter to Longyearbyren to shop any time we want to go," he says proudly, not realizing that the company docks his pay for these excursions.

There's a huge communal dining hall, a forlorn hospital, a school, and a hotel for visitors, with a bar where we buy shots of vodka, as well as a farm on the hill, a summer garden, and an old-fashioned theater on whose stage traditional Russian dances are performed. The women are hefty, and the men—all miners—are black-faced. The pollution from the mine—plumes of black smoke wafting over snowy mountains and ice-littered seas—serves as a reminder that one of our most complex problems is how to balance the needs of humans from developing countries with the need for a healthy planet. To do so, we must make decisions that are all-inclusive and biologically sound, taking human, cultural, and biological elements into consideration instead of looking for economic gain only.


By two o'clock we're onboard the *Noorderlicht* again. A Norwegian fireboat is docked next to us, and a dog—a Siberian husky—is chained up on deck. I look across at him and he at me. I see open snowfields and frozen fjords in his eyes. He sees my claustrophobia. I turn to Ted: "Let's get out of here."

Soon the ruined mountain is behind us. Seal song soaks up

through the hull. We're making our way to Longyearbyren. Ko has to catch a plane. Now that we have our sea legs under us, we can do anything, "as long as the boat is rocking," David Buckland says, laughing. By the time we finish this two-week voyage, we will have traveled 1,020 miles.

Later, we debate the variables having to do with global warming. How much is part of the natural cycle? How much is provoked by human carelessness, idiocy, and greed? In another bay we make concentric circles around seals, reluctant to leave. There are stories of arctic hysteria in humans and animals, and there are also tales of beauty-induced trance. Surely the Sirens were seals. We glide by a branching glacier, its two arms holding a geological knot. Six terns perch on a piece of blue ice, exhausted from their long journey. Soon they'll go to their nest sites and incubate eggs. They have roughly 132 days to nest, hatch out chicks, fledge, and fly again. Now snow begins to fall and will not stop. Ko stands beside me on deck. He is crying. I hold him. I put the headphones with the seal songs to his ear.

# WALRUS

*Shhhhh . . . shhhhh . . . shhhh . . .* The sound of ice hitting the hull. Then a *thonk*. We hit something big. I bolt out of my bunk and go on deck. David is at the helm, and Maaike is standing on the bowsprit looking for ice and signaling to David which way to turn. She gestures one way, then the other. The big wheel spins. Accuracy is necessary; one wrong turn and an iceberg could send us the way of the *Titanic*. I stand on the raised deck behind David. Ice lies on water as far as the eye can see: scattered rhinestones, spiral arms of ice, ice walls and icebergs, and bits of ice that have splintered off larger pieces whose translucent edges are shaped like miniature whales.

On either side of the *Noorderlicht* ivory gulls are taking baths: dunking under the water, shooting up again, lifting their wings, grooming their chests with their beaks. We are headed for Ny-Alesund, an international research center committed to understanding climate change. There's a long night's passage in rough water; by morning we turn eastward into Kongsfjorden.

---

At the Norwegian Polar Institute, we follow Jan to the roof of the building. To the north are snow-covered mountains; to the south, the slow-thawing fjord. "All nations are welcome here," he says. "We have scientists from Norway, Sweden, Russia, Poland, Japan, Denmark, Germany, China, and the United Kingdom, and we're here to support their research. We provide housing, food, guns (for protection from polar bears), snow scooters, weather information, and all kinds of instrumentation and communication possibilities."

Snow falls gently as we stand amidst buzzing instruments. "Our main research now has to do with the changing climate. Here, we study the effects of solar radiation, stratospheric ozone concentrations, global radiation, short- and long-wave radiation, UV radiation, spectral UV, ozone, the long range transport of pollutants, sea ice, the penetration of solar light on ice, and the structure of the melting process and how it's connected to the water beneath." As he talks we gaze at charts of glacial recession.

"We study the concentration of pollutants in arctic animals and the reasons for high concentrations of PCBs in their systems. We're monitoring glacial advances and retreats. While most glaciers are retreating, there's one over here that is surging," he says, pointing. "It advances three meters per day in the summer. But the general trend is a ten percent retreat since the 1960s. And by comparing the 450,000 years of climate history now available to us, we can identify how much anthropogenic influences affect the natural cycles in the ever-changing climate."

One Chinese geophysicist wants to follow a magnetic line from pole to pole; the history of the world could be written there. Another is studying the effect of solar storms on weather, and believes that solar radiation has much more to do with climate change than thought previously. Someone else is taking up the study of flame retardants, their chemical similarity to hormones and their effect on mammals. There's no end to the bad news.

After a sauna in the research center's gym, we count seals hauled out on fjord ice. We're nearing the end of our time in Kongsfjorden. We would continue north if we could, but global warming or not, there's too much ice. We're only seven hundred miles from the North Pole. "We were lucky to get in anywhere at all," Ted confesses. Then with a grin, "We might have had to keep sailing for the rest of our lives."

Late at night two young scientists from the institute come aboard: a Norwegian named Kare, and Sebastian, a serious, dark-haired German geophysicist. "I'm here to study the properties of sea ice," Sebastian says. "I look at it while it is freezing and also when it is thawing, and take samples of the water below to see how thawing or freezing affects things like salinity, density, temperature, nutrients, and sea life. In the 1990s, the climate really changed. It was the time to be here to see that change happen before our eyes. We're looking at climate archives in ice-core samples to see what happened with industrialization, how much human impact is affecting the ice.

There is more work to do to fully understand the process. All the influences and natural variables need a lot more assessment to answer the questions."

We're joined by Andy, the grip from the film crew, and Anna, the cook. Both are drunk. They open beers and pass potato chips. Sebastian continues: "It's too easy to make a snap judgment, to find the sea ice getting thinner and say that it is all human-caused, or simply a part of nature. We are looking for the truth in the complexity. We go out onto the ice and take samples; then we compare what we are seeing with historical ice-data charts. I am looking now at the exact form of the ice edge and at the sediments on the sea floor. The signatures of the sediments are an indication of what has been happening in the world, things like wind carrying dust, smoke, and the extent of volcanic activity. We see how the depositions have been laid down and where they have been disturbed. These are clues to understanding the history of weather, and what is happening now in the way of warming and the possibility of another ice age."

More beers come to the table, and Sebastian leaves. But Kare stays, snuggling with young Sara. "I was a big disappointment to my father," he says. "I dropped out of college. I farmed, I sold vacuum cleaners, I worked in shops, drove taxis, made sausages, sold TVs. Then, I went back to school. I finished my final university exam on a Saturday, and I went to work here on a Monday. I had one day free. It's what I wanted. I love it here; I smile when I go out onto the ice."

———

Andy and Anna are kissing. Her shirt comes undone, and her red bra strap falls from her shoulder. Kare says how hard it is to come to any conclusion about the weather because of all the new influences on it. "There are so many separate disciplines," he says, "and none of us knows what the other one knows. It's hard for us to put it all together."

Anna looks at him and gives him a hug. "Yes, I'm all for getting together with everyone," she says. Kare indulges her embrace. "I'm an atmospheric physicist," he continues. "But the guy next to me might be a biologist, and someone else is a geologist. . . . I think some bad things are happening that will affect our daily lives. The rapid increase in atmospheric carbon dioxide and methane, for example. Everything is pointing upward in terms of warmth. I have two children. Probably they will survive. But maybe diseases will kill all of us first. There are too many people doing things for their own good without thinking of anyone else."

Anna drops cigarette ashes on someone's computer and knocks the satellite phone out of its cradle. She looks at Kare bleary-eyed: "But I cook for everyone. Do you want to know my whale recipe?"

Kare, ignoring her, continues: "We scientists are trying to put our heads together to know what's going on."

Anna continues: "First sauté the whale steaks, and after, make a sauce of olive oil, wine, and butter. That's the recipe we named after the Greenpeace guy . . . what's his name? Watson? Yeah . . . I feed it to him before he knows what it is." Laughter, then Andy pulls her to him. "Darling," she says.

"You should go to bed," Andy tells her. Kare opens another beer. Andy grabs Anna's hand and kisses it. "You look like Zsa Zsa Gabor," he says to her.

"Do I?" she asks dreamily, then smiles and slumps on the table.

Kare continues: "Yeah, for it's hard to know if, just because things are getting hotter, they might not suddenly get cold again. For example, in 1997 we had nine feet of snow on April twenty-eighth in my hometown of Tromsö. But still the planet is warming and the climate is changing fast."

"The totality of life, known as the biosphere to scientists and creation to theologians, is a membrane of organisms wrapped around Earth so thinly it cannot be seen edgewise from a space shuttle, yet so internally complex that most species composing it remain undiscovered. The membrane is seamless. From Everest's peak to the floor of the Mariana Trench, creatures of one kind or another inhabit virtually every square inch of the planetary surface." I'm reading from E. O. Wilson. It's evening. We're under way again but going south. The gray sky is sun-pierced. Glaciers kneel down at water's edge and let their legs break in slapping wind-waves. I don't know why I'm crying. We've become so hardened, and the sea is trying to break us open again. An arctic tern flicks her wings once and soars fast in the direction of an uninhabited island. I like to think that I know her. She was flying above the Beagle Channel at the bottom of the world, and now, since we've both just arrived at latitude 79 degrees north, I'm seeing her again.

Belowdecks, we work at our various projects. Nick has trapped air, fjord water, and light in three separate vessels to take home to his child. David Hinton shoots film of ice-covered seawater, and Val takes the ocean's temperature. Clouds pull across gold mountains and hang motionless, sea ice crumbles, and bare spots on the land begin to show.

Most of us are estranged from what is actually going on all around us. "Nature is the matrix in which the human mind evolved," E. O. Wilson said. "Without it we devolve. Simple as that. We are devolving."


Cold. Cold enough for seawater to freeze. Ice covers our wake. Yet, just north of here, the Gakkel Ridge, a thousand-mile-long slit in the ocean floor, is belching out heat in a long line, what one scientist called "a simmering necklace of volcanoes and hot-water vents that may harbor unique life-forms." While extinctions are occurring at a horrendous, galloping pace, new life-forms are being found, albeit tiny ones. Nevertheless, it might be constructive to ask what we want our world to look like in the future: do we want picoplankton to replace hippos, bears, and ourselves?


We pass slowly out of Kongsfjorden, make a sharp turn south, and enter the strait between Prins Karls Forland and the coast of the main island. We've taken down the sails and proceed under power. The passage is so shallow we have only one meter to spare, and any wrong turn will put us aground. With

Ted at the wheel, we inch along. Maaike and Ward concentrate on navigating. It's silent on deck. Then Maaike yells: "Walrus!"


Our last rite of passage is this: we take the Zodiac to a spit of land where the walrus have hauled out. It's snowing hard and the sea is rough. The film crew are clutching their gear, lifting it up every time a wave crests over the side of the boat. We're wet and it's cold—somewhere around zero—and we have to bale water. Just before reaching shore, Ward spins the boat around and cuts the engine. We paddle backward to keep from getting swamped. Shore consists of six inches of gravel, then a ten-foot-high snowbank up which we have to climb. Waves crash against our legs. We're like lemmings racing to shore. Ted extends a hand down and pulls me up. I flop on the snow like a seal. The Zodiac speeds away.

We walk the length of the spit in blinding snow. Ahead is a lump of something—a blubbery pile of male walruses sleeping at the edge of the sea. Each weighs one to two tons. They are gentle, nuzzling one another with their ivory tusks and scratching their heads with back flippers that look like huge hands. As we approach, they give us the shy, doubtful look of young children, but if we keep our distance, they ignore us altogether.

Marine mammal biologists fear for walrus populations in the Chuckchee, Bering, North Atlantic, and Barents Seas. Retreating and thinning ice is threatening their lives. Walrus can't dive as deep as seals do. They live on benthic animals—mostly shellfish—found where the sea floor is soft and shallow. They need to be near drift ice, which they use as a platform for resting and breeding. But as the Arctic warms, thin floes collapse under them, and the distances between shallow substrates—continental and island shelves—that also have drift ice nearby grow too large.

Females don't have pups until they are five or six, and male walruses don't reach sexual maturity until eight or nine. They need time and ice and food, but warming conditions are often leaving these needs unmet. As sea level rises, continental shelves become too deep for the shallow divers like walruses to use. They are in danger of having no place to feed at all.

We move slowly down-channel through melting brash ice. Ahead, it's all white; there may be too much ice for the *Noorderlicht* to get through. If ice stops us, we'll have to turn around and take the outer route in rough water again. Low clouds obscure the coast. David asks Ted if we'll make it. Ted grins: "We have so far." Sailors don't believe in the future, only in the water in front of them. There is silence on deck. We listen not just for ice, but for the sound of the hull hitting bottom. Five hours later we round the bend into Isfjorden.

Eider ducks fly past, two by two, beating us into Longyear-byren; the fjord ice opens slowly. At EISCAT, a research center on top of a mountain above town, we hear about the fragility of the upper atmosphere, how sensitive it is to environmental changes, about the feedback effect, the million-degree solar corona, the plasma wind and the solar wind streaming from the surface of the sun where it is 6,000 degrees. We are told how coronal mass ejections shoot particles through Earth's magnetic field, about incoherent scatters, electron densities, ion temperature, and velocity; and how solar radiation affects climate change.

Later I lie on the aft deck of the *Noorderlicht* wrapped in a Polartec jacket. In a few hours we'll be flying back to London. In the lower latitudes an unusually hot summer is having its way with cities, people, and crops, and what's left of alpine glaciers. How I dread going back to all that—to night and the domestic violence of green where ice falls down as sweat on foreheads, and loosened hair is rain.

I think of the cool contraption of a glacier's snout breaking apart in the blasting, all-night light of Spitsbergen, of the ice streams coursing off the Greenland ice cap, of the surging Perito Moreno glacier in southern Patagonia. At both ends of the world, the persistent undulations of snowflakes, sands, gravels, gases, and waters are stories held inside ice—recent stories, and ones from long ago. To trace how each snowflake fell, collapsed, became ice, carrying with it the dust, pollens, and pollutions of the day, is in itself more than a life's work.

It cheers me to think of the ice cores from Greenland and

eastern Antarctica all stored together in a very cold library, on shelves made of ice, under an icicle-clad rotunda. The books of ice will be arranged spine out and have names like *North Window, Icepanishad, Burning Ice*, and a newspaper called *The Daily Ice Chronicle*. There will be picture books of early refrigerators lined in rabbit fur, and museums will exhibit "the coldest object in the universe," which is some obscure particle that almost reaches absolute zero. Theories of absolute zero will dominate academia. Our planet will be called not Earth, but *Sila*, the Greenlandic word that means, simultaneously, "weather" and "consciousness."

Parallel worlds, both inner and outer, will be easily recognizable. The archives of consciousness and physical being will be laid out in dioramas displaying smooth and undulating depositions of ice, as well as sonic, seismic, and neurological brain waves. Books made of ice will fill the shelves. The power of climate with its drastic, surefire changes may someday cause our little speck of human life—our edifices, ideas, entanglements, and frailties—to vanish, and the records of what we have been will melt away.

I go below and sleep in my bunk. Sadness melts. Snow returns. In Wyoming the canoe bangs onto the ice and severs the river. In California a canyon wren's song wakes me; her airy, descending notes flutter down to the watery ones of the bearded seal. Hot and cold rivulets of air waft over my head and into my nose and mouth: wrath, peace, wrath, peace. Eyes open. I see wide white nights, blazing snowfalls, tangled love sheets, coarse sand and fine, rising from deep in the water well.

I have no god, no parents, no children. Some days I want to go to Sam's grave, dig him up, and hold him once again. But I don't. Beauty saves me. As for ceremony, it is all around us. It is everything that happens every day. I walk the *sendero* in circle after circle and tend the twig fire of love with no possession, no future, only today and today, one year becoming another. I try to remember the economic lessons of the glacier, the amorous ones of the bearded seal, the terns' hope, the winter river's beauty, and the teachings of Sam.

This world is all ours, belonging to each of us: swan, crane, walrus, wren, dog, muskrat, saxifrage, pine, polar bear, you, me. But too many of us have relinquished our hold on the natural world and turned toward power and the ownership of things. The circuit that binds air to ocean, river to mountain, snowdrift to glacier, ice to water, flows through each of us. We are the vessels that help carry *sila*. Beauty streams through us, inside and out, the way waves and skeins of radiant energy from the sun give us life.

I go on deck. Picoplankton dance, white-cloud mountains fall at my feet. I slip into a harness and clip in. Under full sail and going south, we are slanted hard to starboard. Seawater streams across scuppers. Snow comes down. "It's not a storm, just winter weather lingering," Ted says. Will winter disappear? Will we be deseasoned? Will we have unendurable heat and dwindling water? Will the Greenlanders make a new word out of *summer* that also means "a year"?

No land in sight. Glaucous gulls wheel by, showing their claws. I long for sweet corruption: a sip of tea, a bit of chocolate, Gary's embrace. A patch of cobalt shows briefly before whitening. Who said the abyss was black? Brash ice swishes past the steel hull as if stroking it to a deeper tenderness—one that is inherent in every season, even winter, but is often overlooked. Winter has the first kiss and the last laugh. *Shhh . . . shhh . . . shhh . . .* Breath sweeps mind. Snow erases it.

*Part Six*

# ON COLD CLIFF

*Here where the trail disappears*
*form asks shadow where to.*

—HAN SHAN

# THE BLACK MOON

Hanyen. "Cold Cliff." That's where I'm walking. In Wyoming another winter has arrived. By October 30 three feet of snow had fallen; by November 8 there were four. Now the steps I make to get up on this cliff are canyons and sinks and, in some places, holes that go down so deep they form another set of legs, perhaps the ones these storms walked in on.

Below is a glacier-carved meadow, and beyond, the cordillera's stacked revetments. Since early October walls of white have been drifting. Now the cliff edge is a sculpted cornice and the mountains' granite blades are tearing snow clouds to get back to blue.

I've been snowed in at my cabin for a month. My cell phone only works on this hill, and even then it's iffy. Too often the cold makes the batteries go dead before the call goes through. My pickup is parked three miles away at the paved road. I'm trying to get out, but it's taking a long time. Each day I squeeze more belongings—both clothes and books—into a big Dana backpack, step into snowshoes, and trudge off the moraine, but two round trips—twelve miles a day breaking trail all the way—is all I can manage. The light is gone by four in the afternoon, and one night, as I came in late on snowshoes and floundered in drifting snow, three wolves followed me home.

My neighbors are gone, blizzards sweep through, white dunes sail. Mornings, I tromp down a path between the cabin and my pickup, but snow keeps stacking up and the tracks drift in as soon as they are made. There is hardly a sign of my comings and goings, of my having been here at all.

Red sky at sunrise means more storms to come. But for now there is sun and the world is encased in heavy sparkle. All the way up the mountain, lights are flashing. Sun beats against snow and snow against sun—a one-man percussion band, winter's Morse code tapping out what message?

Smooth slopes, sagebrush, aspen branch, pine needle, barbed wire, fence post—all are spangled. I peer down; the snowflakes that cover a willow leaf are flat blades, radiant wings, pearlescent cloth. Gary was supposed to visit; now he's not coming. I brush my hand across the leaf's surface: clear-cut. The flapping stops, and the light show. The flakes are shorn.


Why does the world keep erasing itself? And who's doing the erasing? Returning to my cabin exhausted, I see that a moose has used my trail. Oh, I'm happy—her deep tracks making curve cuts inside of mine. We don't need conjugal visits, the moose and I. Her unseen presence is enough.

Below Sam's grave the moose's tracks split off from mine

and go north. The pulsing sparkle subsides. The cabin sheds snow from its roof in stiff manes, as if white horses were standing in front of the windows. There is no view.

As I sit quietly, snow scratches air like sand. I bring tea into water with a whisk. Not leaves but powder swirling. This blizzard. I drain the cup. It breaks. The snow around the cabin is green.

Early evening. At Hanyen a heavy-grained dusk encloses the cliff. Under the snow, wild blossoms are shut tight and withered grasses still lie tangled. I think of the terns, flying the Tropic of Capricorn toward Queen Maud Land, thrumming the strings of magnetic-field lines as if playing a guitar. Their flight paths gird the planet north to south, crossing the Holarctic ones of fulmars, the east-west flights of hummingbirds, the round-the-world peregrinations of albatross at *el fin del mundo.*

Not moving. The day decays. Not into snow—it's too cold for that—but into the fast fade of sun-embossed slopes. I face the great wall of mountains. Altar or barricade? Maybe both. Dark envelops me. Then, from behind a peak, something shines, but what? Now I see: *a black moon rises.*

Not quite black but copper all blotched, or else dried blood with mist spraying from it, and the center gone black. *Who rubbed ashes on this face?* There's a tale of a Chinese monk who drowned trying to catch the moon, but what story tells of a moon that has burned?

Up it goes, oh, so smoothly, a spinning rosewood burl rotting to ebony, an ember floating, seeking oxygen with which to fan its own fires. Now I see: it's only a stony globe, a dark seed.

A lunar eclipse occurs when the full moon's tilted orbit enters the Earth's shadow. A horizontal line strings the three pearls of sun-Earth-moon. Earth blocks sun; moon receives shadow. A few of the sun's rays keep scattering forward to tint the moon red. Then they too are blocked as the moon swings slowly into the shade.

Moon is a dropped rock, accidental, moody, receiving only the light that sun deigns to give. Yet its tug is stronger than we are. Who of us can pull out a set of unturned waves, make them break, sweep them back again?

Between is the blue-and-dustbin Earth with her throbbing glaciers, trapped air bubbles, star-beaded skies, rising oceans, and overheated cities hemmed together with cars.

Sun is restless. Four days before this eclipse the most powerful solar eruption ever recorded occurred. The sun swelled and shrank as gases, pulled from the interior, burst at the surface, cooled, and were sucked inward again. It's magnetic-field lines aren't as orderly as Earth's. The sun's lines tangle with superheated plasma and are dragged sideways by ferocious winds until the gaseous knots explode in sunspots and burst through the solar corona in billion-ton clouds of matter, each one big enough to swallow several Earths.

———

I look skyward. "Where is the dark seed which grows the forget-you-plant?" the Japanese poet Sosei wrote in 890. Black tulips might grow from this moon's seed, if it germinated. It does not. The mist dissolves. At midtotality the moon is utterly absorbed by night.

Now black. It was only borrowed light anyway. The 1,382,000-kilometer-long shadow is the thing. It shoots oblivion into everything. I pace the edge of the moraine. The cliff floats and the moon is dead. A river of darkness runs between.

I click on my phone. There's just enough battery time for one short call. My friend Tony answers. He's in the backseat of a car on his way into Manhattan. I ask if he can see the eclipse. He sticks his head out the car window, the New York wind hitting his phone and spurting out of mine. "Yes! Yes! *Fangul!* It's all—" *Click.* The battery goes dead. It's fifteen degrees below zero, and my phone-holding hand is numb.

Far below I see something moving: it's the moose headed up-canyon. Come back! I cry. Use my trail anytime. Before my voice carries across the meadow to her, she's gone. I move down from the moraine. My snowshoes sink. There is no moon. Without it, will the tides stop changing? Will women get pregnant? Will we stop going mad?

Yesterday I read about a bioluminescent sea sponge, the *Euplectella,* which lives in utter darkness at a depth of between five hundred and one thousand feet. Its body is made of light-emitting fibers called spicules, glass cores infused with sodium ions that make it shine. With the light it manufactures inside its own body, the *Euplectella* shines a path forward, then drifts on it to find food. In the abyss, it is its own sun.

There's nothing like that here. Just wolves, bears, moose, elk, coyotes, and humans skulking around, and a moon that has disappeared from sight. Tonight the terns from the Arctic are dropping down from heights of twenty thousand feet to skim the sea surface for fish, before going aloft again. Equatorial night has already closed down fast on their wings; South African light will lift them.

At the cabin I knock down the snow shed from the metal roof. The once-hidden view now reveals only a blank: night plastered on top of night, and no glimpse of the errant moon. In Greenland, before modern times, total darkness brought on psychotic events in arctic foxes, sled dogs, and humans. Running in circles, biting, howling, and hallucinating were common disorders due to mineral, fat, and light deprivation.

I eat a handful of almonds and sit tight. Then something does show: the moon in transit is a bright rind bursting from the lower edge of a globe. As the black patch begins to disappear, the high peaks of the Rockies, crowded together in their secret mountain fastness, light up.

Somewhere deep in the canyon the moose is following a trail and the string lake at her feet takes on silver. It is another kind of moon come down to her, a void describing a full circle, a full circle emptying into a void. She lowers her head, hits the ice hard with her right paddle until water seeps up. Silver floats to her lips. She drinks, then takes the moon's bright promise with her, into the heart of the mountains—all glacier-smoothed granite and hung with moon-spangled ice.

Upstream, pushing into a tangle of willows, she nibbles a few red leaves as the inward-shining light of a blind moon and an imploding sun loosens itself all over the place. Then, dropping to her knees as do I—not to a false god or a real one, but to life itself—the moose surveys her surroundings, lies on her frozen bed, and sleeps.

# LAST CALL

Weeks ago the sandhill cranes circled, practicing flight patterns, getting ready to fly south. Swans huddled in the last patch of open water—a quiet dogleg off a stream. Ice had been growing at the edges of their pond, glazing over water like cataracts. By the time it reached all the way to the center, the cranes, swans, and the last pair of western bluebirds were gone.

Now, as I snowshoe home in silence, the tilted-up, ice-carved fenders of the moraine seem lifeless. Icy winds make my eyes water, or are they real tears? We seem to have forgotten that we can choose how we want the world to be by making transformation possible—from GNP to GNB—from the production of goods to the possibilities of beauty.

Reaching the cabin, I enact the same small rituals: lighting the kerosene lamp, starting a fire in the woodstove, making tea, lighting a stick of incense for Sammy.

Some days I wonder why I'm here, why I'm anywhere, and what kind of "weather" and whose flight paths keep all the random bits of life from flying apart. It still astounds me that neural patterns "describe" events in temporal succession until an image appears in the mind's eye, then another and another.

Narrative begins that way, and symphony, and the whole juicy mess of the human condition. Neural weather is wild, and so is the mind of river, ocean, blizzard, and moraine.

Lately, when I'm very tired, I've felt neurological shifts—nothing alarming, just a brain lesion being scratched, or the part of my life relegated to lighting-induced amnesia trying to escape its blank cage. On those days I make coffee, strong. It looks like the night, and I drink it down. Outside, in the silence left behind by migrating birds, I listen for the B-flat of a black hole squeezing and heating galactic gas, pushing it into concentric ripples 35,000 light-years apart until a sound is emitted, a long-held note fifty-seven octaves below middle C. But I hear nothing and go back inside.

To live remotely—though sometimes strangled by loneliness—to be pursued by wolves or bears that might eat me, or bulldozed down by an angry moose, prickles my skin, causes jubilation, fast heartbeats, and whoops of joy. Mornings I compose thought from birdsong; evenings I count droplets, like money, in rising mist. Here, and everywhere, the primordial overrides what we are conditioned to think, feel, perceive, and believe. I once had a dog whose breathing moved the world.

Grasping and rejecting—there's been plenty of that in my life. But here the real keeps driving into the false. Morning comes. Night comes. Morning returns.

I pack the last of my books and clothes and step into my snowshoes. Standing in the doorway, I bow to the stacked-up "standing dead" pine trees that make this house, then to Sammy in his grave. Sideslipping down a cornice of snow onto an old track—the one I've been trying to keep packed hard for two months—I begin the three-mile jaunt to my pickup truck. The snowshoes still sink, but the hidden track beneath is firm and it holds me.

Winter's embrace is offered this way. It is a long arm— ephemeral, hidden, and oddly sturdy. Far above are the bird paths that bind pole to continent, to island, to moraine, to pole. I make my own feeble track across wind-hardened snowdrifts and abandoned swan ponds, and wonder how much longer the season of winter will exist and if we'll survive. Behind me is the moose trail entering winter's oblivion, and the meadow, a thousand acres wide, its snowy expanse carved by wind *en cabochon*—in fluid curves instead of facets.

The claws of my snowshoes scrape across hard crust and curds of fallen snow fall like little universes from the aluminum frames. I dig in hard with my poles and wonder if there's a black moon tumbling beneath this planet that is, like a tern, caught in shadow and pining for light.

Wind drives fine-grained snow before my feet. Gaby is panting now, or is it a smile? Ahead, sun shafts light into the mountains and another storm mounds up behind. All I know is this—and maybe I don't know it at all: the winter world is the one where the cold flame of passion is used to set ourselves free from desire.

NOTES AND SOURCES

Like a heart patient who does not know if she will live through the night, I find myself pondering the future of ice, which is really the future of life. Will life continue, or have we put into action a global machinery that has already destroyed too much and cannot be stopped? In this book—a love affair with winter—ice has been the canary. To educate yourself about climate change, its causes, and how it affects us biologically and culturally, is easy and simple, and there is no excuse for ignorance.

The following easy-to-find Internet sites will inform the reader of breaking news about all aspects of climate change, global warming, sudden cooling, the North Atlantic Drift, rising sea levels, water-world emergencies, desertification, the effects of pollutants on climate, ecosystem shifts, habitat fragmentation, species extinctions, the spread of disease, the early onset of spring, the causes of severe weather in temperate climates, the death of coral reefs, the melting of the last ice sheets, the changes in global atmosphere and ocean-circulation systems, and pollution transport systems, among many other topics.

The very best science magazines are available online as well as in print. They are indispensable, since no published book can keep up with news about climate change. They are: nature.com, scientificamerican.com; sciencenews.com; newscientist.com; peopleandplanet.net, and sciencemag.org; as well as the online services of NASA, NOAA, and the EPA.

Other valuable sites can be found by using search engines and specific sites. The ones I used daily were: SIRS, Google News—climate change, Yahoo, NOAA, NRDC, Climateark, Worldwildlife, and Questia, among many others. All these will lead the reader to many more links about the changing environment.

The following books were invaluable: E. O. Wilson, *The Future of Life;* Paul Mayewski and Frank White, *The Ice Chronicles; The Random House Atlas of Bird Migration;* David Allen Sibley, *The Sibley Guide to Bird Life and Behavior;* E. C. Pielou, *A Naturalist's Guide to the Arctic;* Peter Marchand, *Life in the Cold;* James Halfpenny and Roy Douglas Ozanne, *Winter: An Ecological Handbook;* Paul Ehrlich et al., *The Birder's Handbook;* Allan Savory with Jody Butterfield, *Holistic Management;* Carl Safina, *The Eye of the Albatross;* Bernd Heinrich, *Winter World;* Ralph Waldo Emerson, *Essays;* Derek Walcott, *Omeros;* Suzuki Bokushi, *Snow Country Tales;* Muso Soseki, *Sun at Midnight;* Red Pine, trans., *Poems of the Masters;* Charles Frazier, *Cold Mountain;* Antonio Damasio, *The Feeling of What Happens;* James Welch, *Fools Crow;* Gladys Reichard, *Navaho Religion;* Rockwell Kent, *Voyaging;* Charles Darwin, *The Voy-*

*age of the* Beagle; Colin McEwan et al., *Patagonia;* and Fridtjof
Mehlum, *The Birds and Mammals of Svalbard.*

In addition were the conversations with biologists, clima-
tologists, ornithologists, and geographers I met during my
travels. Among them were Kristen Larson, George Divoky,
Ko de Korte, Paul Mayewski, Allan Savory, and, especially,
Brendan Kelly, at the University of Alaska, who elucidated
quandaries when no one else could.

Every conversation we can have about the beauty and vigor
of the world and the damage being done to it is vitally important. In so doing, we pay homage to what Ted Hoagland calls
the world's "infinite harmonious unruliness."

Love life first, then march through the gates of each season;
go inside nature and develop the discipline to stop destructive
behavior; learn tenderness toward experience, then make decisions based on creating biological wealth that includes all people, animals, cultures, currencies, languages, and the living
things as yet undiscovered; listen to the truth the land will tell
you; act accordingly.

# ACKNOWLEDGMENTS

Heartfelt thanks to those who assisted me during the writing of this book. First, to Marty Asher of Vintage Books, who called me in my winter-bound tent to ask if I'd write it; to my editor, Dan Frank, whose enthusiasm and vision have inspired me for twenty years. To Rita Donham and Jaimie Burgess, my Wyoming neighbors, deep thanks. To John and Lucy Fandek for midwinter shelter and an unforgettable canoe trip through ice; to Betsy Greenwood and Tom Brown, Maggie Miller, Rick and Jennifer Ridgeway, Malinda and Yvon Chouinard, Happy and Ken Price, and Jan Andrews, all of whom lent me their homes, provided showers, food, and, most important, friendship. Throughout the writing of this book, Mark Domek was single-handedly building a beautiful cabin for me, which I now happily inhabit. Thanks to his family, Pat Poletti, Callie, and Sara. I'm grateful to my childhood friend and architect Karl G. Smith, who put the cabin on paper; to Huntley Dornan, who helped with research; to Michael Wenger at San Francisco Zen Center, an extraordinary friend who talked to me about circles and ceremony; to Barbara Wenger; and to Bill Porter—Red Pine—for his marvelous translations and commentaries.

As always, I'm indebted to my teacher, Chogyam Trungpa Rinpoche. Thanks to my dear pal in London, David Buckland, and his Cape Farewell Project that took me to Spitsbergen; to Ko de Korte and all those who sailed on the *Noorderlicht;* to my sister Galen Wood, and to Mary Hebner, Tamara Asseyev, and Hillary Hauser, who provide moral support wherever I am. To Robin, Jim, and Crister Brady, who helped with Sam; to Brent and Patty at the Pinedale Vet Clinic; to Annick Smith and Bill Kittredge, friends and neighbors during stints in Montana; to John McGough, who has given my horses a home; to William Gilchrist, who took care of Sam and Gaby during my long absences; to my friend William Merwin for his poems and translations; and to my mentor, Edward Hoagland. In memory of those recently lost: Louis Netzer, Bunker Sands, James Welch, and John Lewis Hopkin, who gave me my first dog, Rusty; and to the memory of canine friends who "went over the ridge" during the writing of this book: Sam, his sister Yaki, and his friend Chester. And to Gary Delp, my love and thanks.

Printed in the United States
by Baker & Taylor Publisher Services